AWARD-WINNING QUILTS

and How To Make Them

JUDY FLORENCE

Cover Design: Ann Eastburn
Interior Layout: Anthony Jacobson

Photographs: Jim Christoffersen

Library of Congress Catalog
Card Number 85-050661

ISBN 0-87069-454-5

10 9 8 7 6 5 4 3 2 1

Published by

Wallace-Homestead Book Company
580 Waters Edge
Lombard, Illinois 60148

This book is dedicated with gratitude and affection to my sister Jean.

Contents

Introduction

As you page through *Award-Winning Quilts*, you will discover quilt patterns that cover a variety of styles and techniques. Whether you favor appliqué or have a propensity for piecing, you're apt to find at least one or more patterns that appeal to you. Each quilt reflects a different technique, style, or design idea. In addition, the range of difficulty is appropriate for both beginning and experienced quiltmakers.

You might begin with the simple pieced-panel wall quilts, such as Spring and Holiday. Experienced quiltmakers could try the more detailed patterns of Sampler or the appliqué in Orange Basket Medallion. Both elementary and intricate quilting designs are included for borders and background areas.

The quilts also include a variety of techniques. There are two pieced quilts (Triangles and Rainbow Patch), two combinations of appliquéd and pieced (Orange Basket and Sampler), and two quick-pieced (Spring and Holiday).

Several quilt styles are covered. There are two "scrap-bag" quilts (Triangles and Rainbow Patch) and one sampler pattern. Two patterns are modified whole-cloth, and one medallion pattern is included. Although the Orange Basket Medallion may appear complicated, it is basically constructed with traditional blocks and the familiar patterns of Basket of Oranges, Trip Around the World, and Jacob's Ladder.

These six seasonal quilts are the result of some of my experimentation with new techniques and styles. My personal quiltmaking revolves around a continual desire to try new ideas and search for new solutions to old problems. I find that I rarely repeat a quilt pattern (unless by commission or request). When faced with a new opportunity or fresh design idea, I usually venture on to another quilt project.

For instance, I designed Spring and Holiday as small pieces that could be assembled quickly and which, when completed, would show the hand quilting to advantage. I wanted a piece that looked quilted, with no doubt about it; where the hand quilting was the focal point, but not so elaborate and time-consuming as to discourage a beginner. The modified whole-cloth panels in Spring and Holiday help accomplish this. They can be assembled quickly, and you can be quilting by the second day. The stitches, shadows, and relief of the finished piece will say "quilted!"

The pattern for Orange Basket incorporates traditional patterns into a medallion setting. My goal was to discover the options and effects of using several print and solid fabrics throughout the blocks and borders. I found that the cutting and placement of tiny squares, diamonds, trapezoids, triangles, and multiple borders provided an array of options: In which direction should the baskets be placed? On the square? On the diagonal? How should the ladder be set? Against the borders? Radiating from the center?

The entire process of experimentation with alternative layouts and settling on final choices is what made Orange Basket Medallion a delightful project for me. You can try it, too. Depending on your willingness to experiment and your personal preferences, you might create a design that you (or anyone else) had not anticipated.

And so it was with the other quilts. A desire to work in soft rainbow hues led to the Rainbow Patch crib quilt. Holiday is the product of a request for a wall hanging with a festive seasonal theme.

How could I transform the spring feeling into fabric? How could I quilt to best complement pieced light/dark scrap triangles? How could I incorporate equal amounts of piecing and appliqué into a quilt? These and numerous other ideas and questions each sparked another quilt pattern.

The result is a diversity of designs that cannot be categorized by one generic name. Each is distinct from the next. Whether your inclination is tradition or innovation, there is a pattern for you. Sit back and read through the How to Use This Book section. Then select the designs that appeal to you, and experience the pleasures of quilting.

How to Use This Book

The patterns and designs in this book are arranged according to the seasons of the year, beginning with Spring and ending with Holiday. I have included three wall hangings (crib-size quilts) that depict seasonal themes, and three bed-size quilts of various other patterns. A separate chapter is devoted to each quilt. Each chapter includes a commentary, directions, and patterns.

The commentary tells about the quilt and may also include comments on the versatility of the pattern.

The directions contain complete instructions and diagrams, including the finished size, a list of required fabric and supplies, and step-by-step guidelines for cutting, assembly, quilting, and finishing.

The patterns are full size and include more than twenty original quilting designs.

The directions assume a general knowledge of the basics of piecing and appliqué. Special instructional materials that pertain to several of the quilts are given in the Appendix section. Look there for tips on precision piecing, how to prepare for quilting, how to make your own quilting designs, and quilt binding tips.

For general information on quiltmaking techniques, additional pattern ideas, and sources for inspiration, nostalgia or history, see the recommended references in the Bibliography.

1

Spring

When the winter doldrums drag on into February and March, it's time to think about a quilt project like Spring. This pattern is an excellent choice for both beginners, who will appreciate the simplicity, and experienced quilters. There are no templates to mark or cut, and the top can be easily and quickly assembled by machine. Experienced quilters will appreciate the opportunity to polish their quilting skills without first spending a lot of time on piecing and appliqué.

Since the pattern requires minimal marking and cutting of fabric pieces, the top and borders can be cut and assembled in one day. Within a matter of hours, you can be hand quilting.

Spring also offers opportunity for creativity. You may try some of your own quilt designs, such as a decorated egg, a bluebird, or a bird's nest. For a crib quilt, try shapes of a bunny, duck, rocking horse, rattle, or balloon. Other suggestions include quilted letters of the alphabet, or geometric shapes such as circles, diamonds, triangles, and hexagons.

Experiment with color. You may select colors that match your decor or expand on your favorite hue. For the border and binding, you may select pure white fabric instead of the natural unbleached muslin.

Spring can be enlarged from a wall hanging to a twin bed covering. To do so, increase the length of the cross-panels from 25″ to 40″, double the number of panels, and use 4″ borders. The finished quilt will be 64″ × 94″, which is ample for a twin bed. The quilting designs may be repeated or complemented with others of your choice.

The selection and coordination of fabrics in soft, solid colors may be a treat or a trial. If you have access to shops that carry an abundant range of colors in cotton solids, the mixing and matching will be a delight. If, however, it is necessary to go to every store in the vicinity and you still do not find the colors you want (which is often my experience), I recommend ordering from swatch sets through a reliable mail-order firm. I have done this for several of my quilts and experienced both prompt and courteous service. In addition, the fabrics are high quality and the color options number in the hundreds.

I originally designed Spring as a piece to attract would-be quilters. The patterns in Spring are not complex, so the satisfaction in completing a hand-quilted project is easily realized. Here is proof that quilt designs do not have to be intricate and formidable to be attractive.

Directions

Finished Size. 35″ × 45″.

Materials. Fabric (44″/45″ cotton or cotton/polyester blends):

- Medium blue solid: 5/8 yard (outer borders and one center panel)
- Dark blue solid: 5/8 yard (middle borders and one center panel)
- Cream solid: 1 1/8 yards (inner borders and binding)
- 1/4 yard each of five other solid colors in a range of blues and greens (for center panels)

Backing: 1 1/2 yards of good-quality unbleached muslin

Batting: 36″ × 46″ bonded polyester

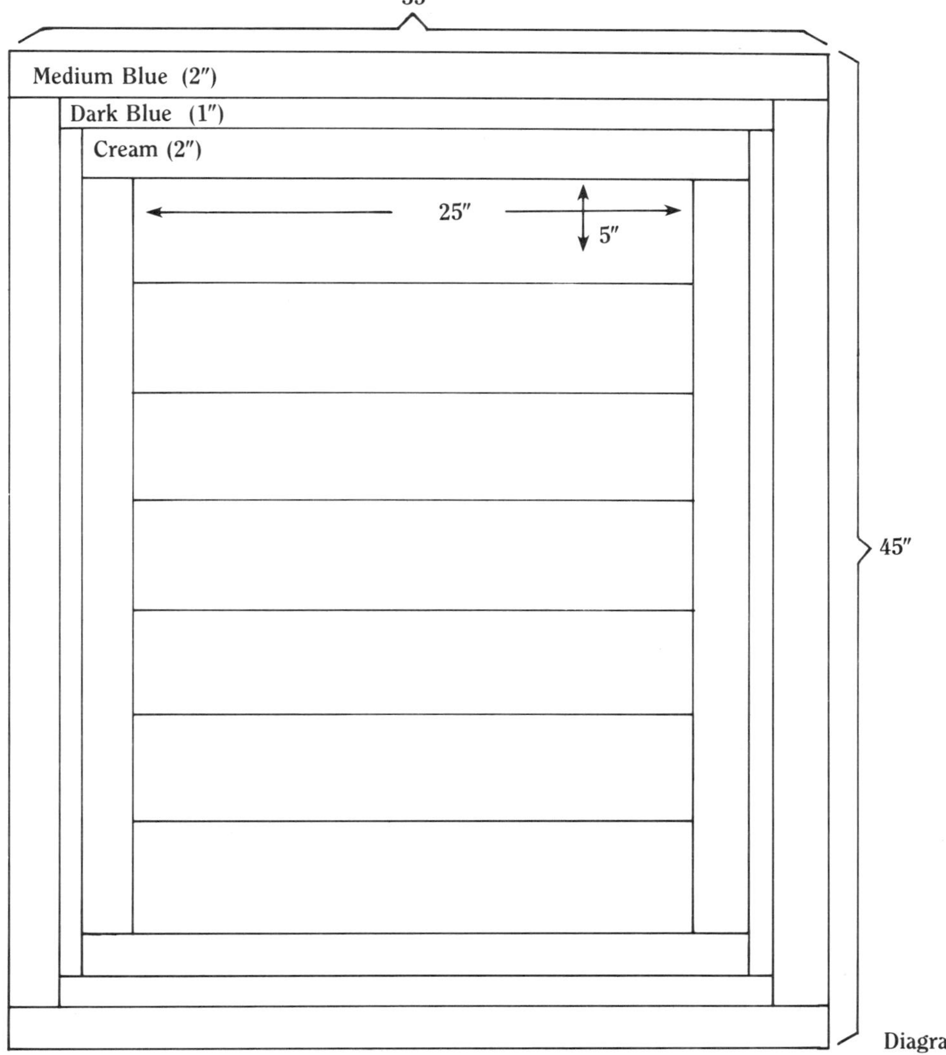

Diagram 1

Other supplies. 4½ yards of tan double-faced ⅛″ wide satin ribbon, sewing thread to match fabrics, one spool of natural-color quilting thread, scissors, washable marking pencil or soap chip, ruler, cardboard or plastic for quilting templates, sewing machine, pins, thread for basting, frame or hoop for quilting, quilting needles, thimble, iron, and (optional) rotary cutter and mat.

Cutting. Seam allowances (¼″ wide) are included on all border and panel measurements. Add about 6″ to the length of each border measurement if you wish to miter the corners. All borders and panels must be cut on the crosswise grain of the fabric, as there will not be enough fabric in the recommended yardages to cut along the lengthwise grain. Cut the following, being sure to cut the borders first.

Cream color (inner borders): Cut two side borders 2½″ × 35½″. Cut two end borders 2½″ × 29½″.

Dark blue (middle borders) from ⅝ yard piece: Cut two side borders 1½″ × 39½″. Cut two end borders 1½″ × 31½″. Cut one panel 5½″ × 25½″.

Medium blue (outer borders) from ⅝ yard piece: Cut two side borders 2½″ × 41½″. Cut two end borders 2½″ × 35½″. Cut one panel 5½″ × 25½″.

From each of the other five blue and green fabrics, cut a panel 5½″ × 25½″ (this includes ¼″ seam allowances).

Assembly. Arrange the blue and green panels in a layout that balances the value and intensity of the colors. With right sides together, pin and then stitch the long sides of each panel in ¼″ seams. Press the seams toward the bottom. Join the borders to the center panels, beginning with the inner cream color border. For each border, attach the sides first, then the ends. See Diagram 1. Press all seams toward the outside.

Quilting. Make templates of the seven Spring quilt designs (kite, wind, birdhouse, shamrock, umbrella, mortarboard, and tulip). Divide each center panel into five 5″ squares, marking lightly with a soap chip or washable marker. Center the quilting design in each square and mark lightly around it, filling in any details such as the lines on the kite, umbrella, and shamrock. Mark five designs on each panel.

Cut a piece of unbleached muslin about 39″ × 49″ for the back of the quilt. Place this piece right side down on a flat surface and layer the batting and then the quilt top (right side up) over it. Carefully pin or baste the three layers together. (*See* Appendix B: How to Prepare for Quilting.) Using a frame or hoop, quilt the central designs and lines between the designs, along the crosswise seams, and across the three borders as shown in Diagram 2. Diagonal lines should be 2½″ apart. Remove the basting.

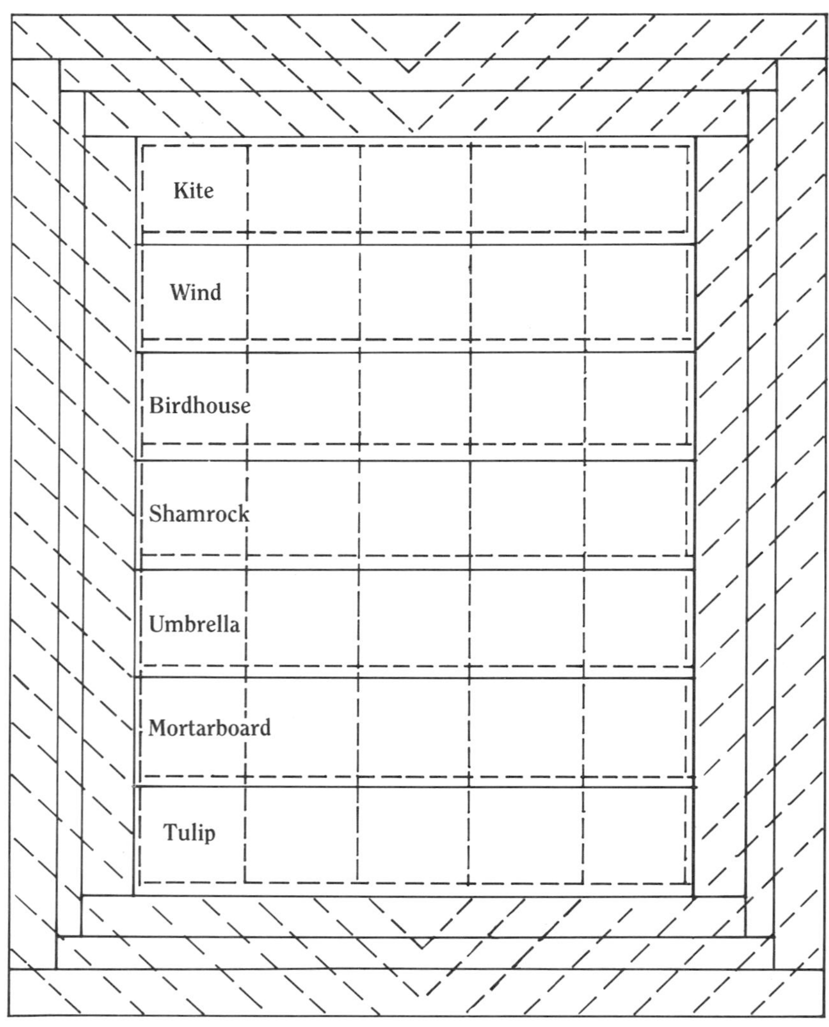

Diagram 2

Finishing. From the remaining cream fabric, cut bias strips 3″ wide and piece them to a sufficient length to border the quilt (about 5 yards). Fold the bias in half lengthwise with the wrong sides together. Pin the binding to the quilt top with the raw edges flush. Stitch a 1/4″ seam through all layers. Turn the folded edge of the binding to the quilt back and whipstitch it to the back.

From the 1/8″ double-face satin ribbon, cut twenty 7″ lengths. Fold into bows (see Diagram 3) and tack to each of the following quilt designs: kite, birdhouse, umbrella, and flower.

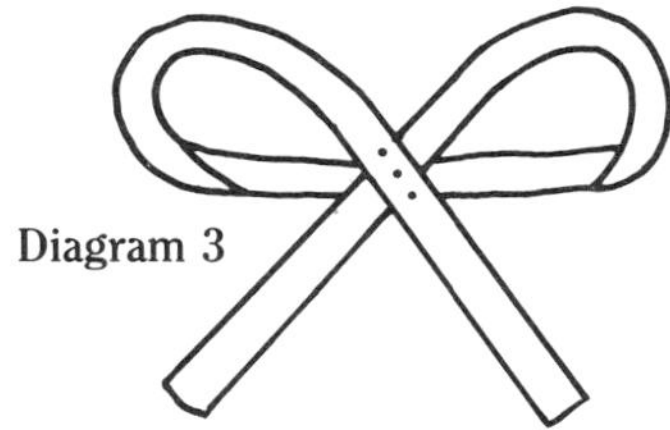

Diagram 3

2

Triangles

Triangles is an excellent scrap-bag quilt. In fact, that's exactly where I found it. The completed top was nestled among sundry fabrics in a box of scraps I purchased at a neighborhood auction.

At first glance, it was not very impressive. But a second examination from a distant perspective revealed an overall graphic design that was simple, yet strong. The placement of light triangles and dark triangles is effective and gives the quilt its natural appeal. Principles used in construction of the familiar Log Cabin pattern and its variations are applied in Triangles.

Besides being visually appealing, Triangles is easy to assemble, and economical, too. There is only one pattern piece, and the fabric can come from your own accumulation of fabric scraps.

Almost anything goes in this quilt. Any lightweight or medium-weight woven fabric made from cotton or a blend of cotton is suitable. Plaids, checks, small prints, solids, florals, geometrics, and dots add character. As long as a fabric can be designated either "light" or "dark," it is appropriate. Witness the wide range of fabrics used in the color photograph.

The most difficult fabric decision you make may be whether to call a scrap light or dark. Here is what I suggest: Gather all fabric scraps together and separate them one by one into piles of light and dark. If in doubt, hold the fabric a short distance away. Or squint to get an overall impression. Aim for an equal number of scraps in each pile.

Random layout of the triangles is another key to the overall effect. Don't try to pair fabrics by color, tone, or motif. You'll have better results if you don't let the fabrics or your personal color sense interfere.

A choice of simple quilting lines also makes this quilt attractive for beginners. There are no complicated designs to mark and stitch. All quilting lines can easily be marked with a long straightedge and marking pencil. Double diagonal quilting lines are placed for ease of quilting; the frequency of quilting through seams and bulky areas has been minimized. All quilting lines run on the bias of the fabric, giving a greater "relief" to the work.

Selection of a dark or medium/dark fabric for binding tends to hold the work together and frame the triangles. I chose a small vintage print similar to one of the scraps within the quilt. You might select a fabric that reflects the flavor of your combination of scraps. In fact, you might prefer to wait until your top is assembled to make your binding choice.

Triangles can be enlarged by adding more rows of pieced triangles or a wide border. For a double quilt (80″ × 95″), add three rows and two more columns of pieced triangles. For a queen-size (90″ × 105″), add five rows and four columns.

If you're ready to face your scrap pile head-on, Triangles is a good choice. No trips to a fabric store are required. Your scrapbag will shrink, and you will have added a charming quilt to your collection.

Directions

Finished Size. 70″ × 80″.

Materials. Fabric (44″/45″ lightweight woven cotton or cotton blends):

Dark or medium/dark scrap fabrics to total about 3¼ yards (see Pattern A for the approximate minimum scrap size)

Light or medium/light scrap fabrics to total about 3¼ yards (see Pattern A for the approximate minimum scrap size)

Backing: 5½ yards of good-quality muslin

Batting: 72″ × 90″ bonded polyester

Binding: 1 yard of dark print

Other supplies. Sewing thread, two spools of natural-color quilting thread, plastic or cardboard for template, scissors, marking pencils, quilting needles, thimble, pins, long ruler, soap chips, iron, and hoop or frame for quilting.

Cutting. From heavy plastic or cardboard, make a triangle template from Pattern A. From dark and medium/dark scraps, cut 224 triangles, adding ¼″ seam allowances all around each piece. (For machine-piecing, include the ¼″ seam allowance on the template.) From light and medium/light scraps, cut 224 triangles, adding seam allowances all around. This will produce a total of 448 triangles for the quilt top.

Assembly. With right sides together, join a light triangle and a dark triangle along the longest edge in a ¼″ seam. For hand-piecing, join from point to point on the marked seam line. (For machine-piecing, seams may be joined from raw edge to raw edge.) Continue joining paired triangles into squares for a total of 224 pieced squares. Press seams toward the darker triangle.

To assemble one-fourth of the quilt top, place seven pieced squares side by side, with a light triangle toward the top and a dark triangle toward the bottom to form Row 1 (see Diagram 1). With right sides together, join the squares in short vertical seams to make one long unit (35″ × 5″, excluding seam allowances). Set Row 1 aside and repeat for Rows 2 through 8. Then join Row 1 to Row 2 in a long horizontal seam. Continue joining Rows 3 through 8 to complete one-fourth of the quilt top. (See Diagram 2.) Make three similar units for the other quarter-sections of the quilt. Then join the four units to make a top measuring 70″ × 80″.

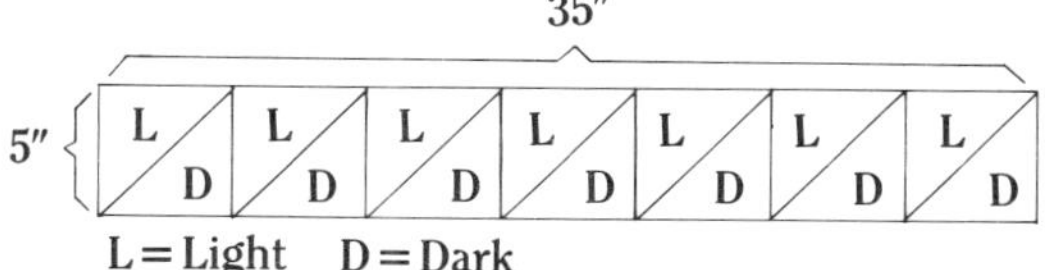

Diagram 1: Row 1 piecing for Triangles

Quilting. From the 5½ yard muslin fabric, cut two 84″ lengths. Keep one intact (about 42″ wide) and split the other into two widths (about 21″ each). Using a ¼″ seam, join a split width to either side of the intact center panel. Press seams toward the outside.

Place quilt backing right side down. Spread batting over it. Place the quilt top over the batting, right side up. Pin or baste the three layers together (see Appendix B: How to Prepare for Quilting).

Mark paired diagonal quilting lines about 3″ apart (as shown in Diagram 3), using a long ruler or yardstick and washable marking pencil or soap chip. Quilt along all marked lines.

Finishing. Trim the quilt batting to ½″ larger than the quilt top. (This will allow for filler in the binding.) Trim the quilt back to match the top. Make bias binding from the 1 yard of dark print fabric (see Appendix D: How to Calculate, Make, and Apply Continuous Bias Binding). Attach binding to the quilt front in a ¼″ seam through all layers. Turn and whipstitch it to the quilt back.

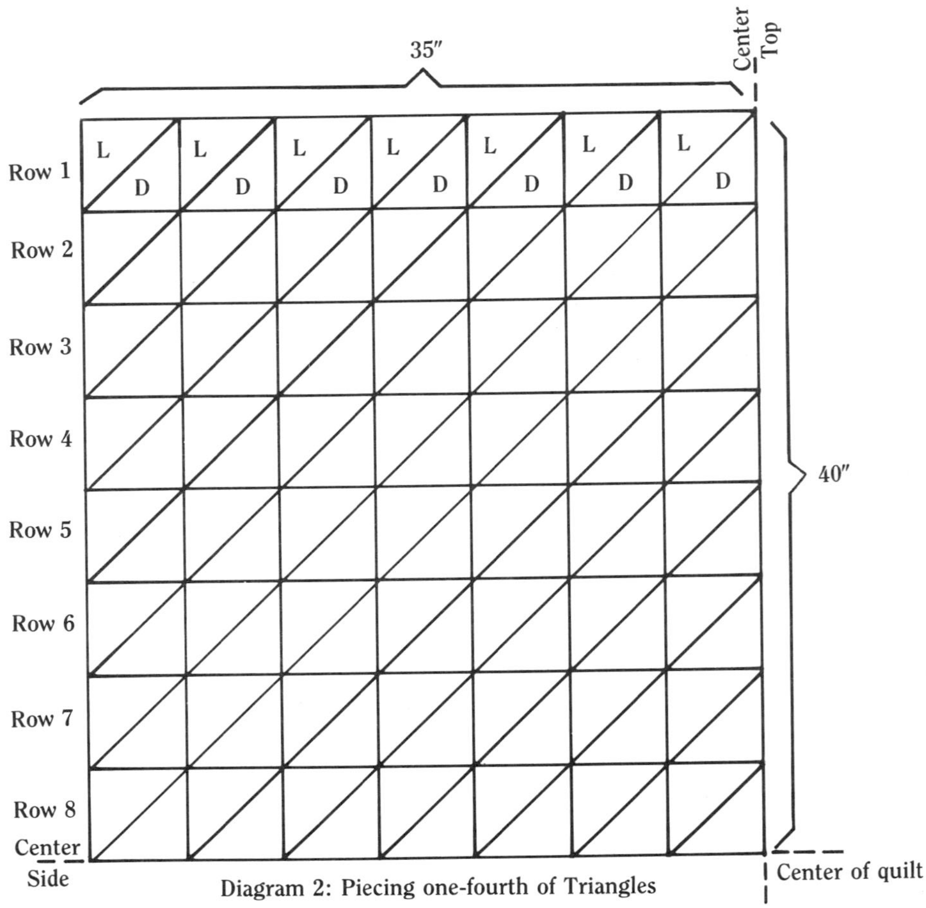

35″

Center
Top

Row 1	L D	L D	L D	L D	L D	L D	L D
Row 2							
Row 3							
Row 4							
Row 5							
Row 6							
Row 7							
Row 8							

40″

Center
Side

Center of quilt

Diagram 2: Piecing one-fourth of Triangles

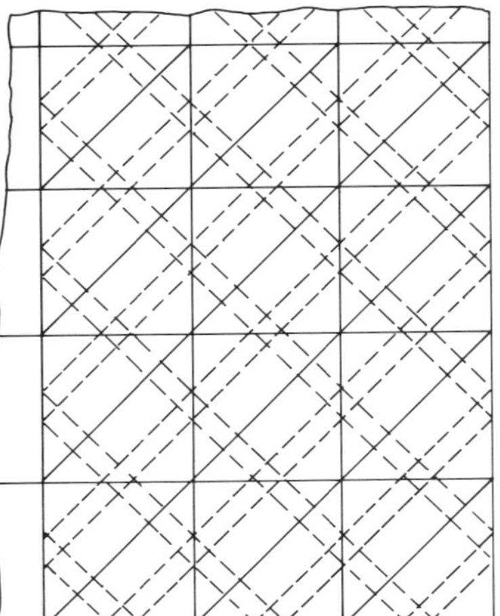

Diagram 3: Suggested quilting for Triangles

3

Sampler

In recent years, the Sampler concept has become popular among quiltmakers, particularly for beginners. Samplers offer the variety of patterns that allows for introduction to the three main facets of quiltmaking: piecing, appliqué, and quilting. I have used this sampler pattern, or its variations, in several beginning and intermediate quiltmaking classes.

An attractive feature of Sampler is the mixture of pieced and appliquéd blocks. My quilt features six of each. Here is the opportunity to try your hand at both techniques, using patterns that are fairly elementary. The piecing is not intricate, and the appliqué portions are not difficult.

Because the Sampler is constructed in a block-by-block method, it can easily be adapted to quilt-as-you-go or lap-quilting, if that is your preference. Each block can be quilted individually and later joined with the latticework and borders for a completed quilt.

Any of your favorite patterns may be substituted in the blocks. All the given patterns are for 14″ squares. If your substitute choice is nine-patch, four-patch, five-patch, or an eight-point star derivative, the templates that are included in the pattern section can be used. To substitute other pieced blocks, you will need to draft them to a 14″ square.

Another option is to select one or just a few of your favorite patterns and repeat them throughout the quilt. One overall pattern is acceptable. If you are enamored with the LeMoyne star, make an entire quiltful. If appliqué is your preference, experiment with a mixture of dahlias, Dresdens, and flower gardens. Try placing the same pattern in the four corners to lend unity to the top. Or start with the shoo-fly and variable star and complement them with other nine-patch patterns of your choice. A selection of star pattern variations would be effective.

You may increase the number of fabrics used – particularly the number and variety of prints. I have used the bare minimum of fabrics – a light, a dark, and a print. The resulting effect is simple and uncomplicated, but possibly uninteresting to many quilters. Addition of a second or third print, particularly if it is a medium, bold, or border print, will enrich the quilt and improve its textural impact. Use of more fabrics increases your possibilities for design as well. More is not always better in fabric selection, but in this case it certainly allows more room for personal expression.

The block-by-block layout of Sampler contributes flexibility in size. It can be altered to double-bed size by changing the narrow outer borders to wide ones. A queen-size quilt can be created by adding eight blocks. A total of six blocks will make a crib/youth size quilt or wall hanging, ideal for beginning quilters who prefer to embark on a smaller project.

Most of the quilting designs are elementary. The only quilting within the blocks is around the pieces, close to the seam. This in-the-ditch method of quilting heightens the relief between shapes and colors. If you prefer a more decorative touch, use an outline stitch approximately ¼″ from the edges of the pieces (just wide enough to clear the seam allowances), or add a decorative motif in each block, such as a seashell or fish in the ship square, or a bouquet of flowers with the girl.

Placing and marking continuous interlocking rings in the outer border may be the most challenging part of Sampler. I suggest that you begin by placing a ring at each corner and at the center of each of the sides, top, and bottom (find the center by folding the quilt top in half in both directions). Next, mark interlocking rings, working from each corner to the center side, making any necessary adjustments along the way.

The latticework is much easier to mark and stitch. I call this shape the "ax head." Others call it the apple core, spool, spindle, or beggar's patch. (One quilting friend refers to it as the 'crotch' design, which is as accurate as any description. I still prefer ax head.) I didn't design or use the shape with an ax head in mind. It is simply the shape that fell out of the center of the interlocking ring template when I cut it. I discovered that it was small enough to fit comfortably on the 3″ latticework. Placement was not a problem, since three units fit nicely along the sides of each block and one unit fits at the intersections.

If you choose to make a sampler quilt, you will be pleased with its adaptability and room for expression. I have listed some sources for pattern substitutions in the Bibliography.

Directions

Finished Size. 66″ × 83″ (twelve 14″ blocks)

Materials. Fabric (44″/45″ cotton or cotton blend):

Dark: 2½ yards (for latticework and throughout blocks)

Light: 4 yards (for background squares, borders, and throughout blocks)

Print: 1½ yards

Backing: 6 yards of dark fabric (includes enough for binding)

Batting: 72″ × 90″ bonded polyester

Other supplies. Sewing thread, thread for appliqué, two spools of quilting thread, plastic or cardboard for templates, scissors, marking pencils, quilting needles, thimble, pins, long ruler, iron, soap chips, and hoop or frame for quilting.

Cutting. See Diagrams 23 and 24 for the light and dark fabric layouts. ¼″ seam allowances are included on the border, latticework, and background square measurements.

Light fabric:

Cut two side borders 6½″ × 71½″.

Cut two end borders 6½″ × 66½″.

Cut six squares 14½″ × 14½″ for the appliqué blocks (Six-Point Star, Sunbonnet Sue, Overall Jim, Dahlia, Grandmother's Flower Garden, and Dresden).

Dark fabric:

Cut five cross-lattices 3½″ × 54½″.

Cut sixteen short strips 3½″ × 14½″.

Make plastic or cardboard templates for pattern pieces numbered S-1 through S-29 (S stands for Sampler). Cut pieces for the twelve blocks according to the following chart, adding ¼″ seams around each piece.

Shoo-fly.

S-1: Cut four light.
S-2: Cut four light, four print.
S-3: Cut four dark, five print.

Six-Point Star.

S-4: Cut three dark, three print.
S-5: Cut six dark, six print.

Variable Star.

S-1: Cut four light, one print.
S-6: Cut four light, four dark, eight print.

Sunbonnet Sue.

S-7: Cut one print.
S-8: Cut one dark.
S-9: Cut one dark.
S-10: Cut one dark.
S-11: Cut one dark.

Irish Chain.

S-12: Cut eight light, five dark, twelve print.

Overall Jim.

S-13: Cut one dark.
S-14: Cut one print.
S-15: Cut one dark.
S-16: Cut two print.
S-17: Cut two dark.
S-18: Cut two dark.

Old Maid's Puzzle

S-19: Cut two dark.
S-20: Cut four light.
S-21: Cut ten light, six print.

Dahlia.

S-22: Cut one light.
S-23: Cut six dark.
S-24: Cut six print.

LeMoyne Star.

S-25: Cut four dark, four print.
S-26: Cut four light.
S-27: Cut four light.

Grandmother's Flower Garden.

S-28: Cut one light, six dark, 12 print.

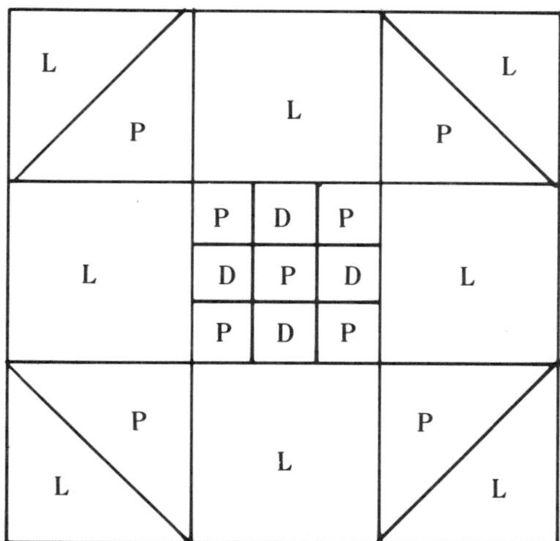

Diagram 1: Shoo-Fly

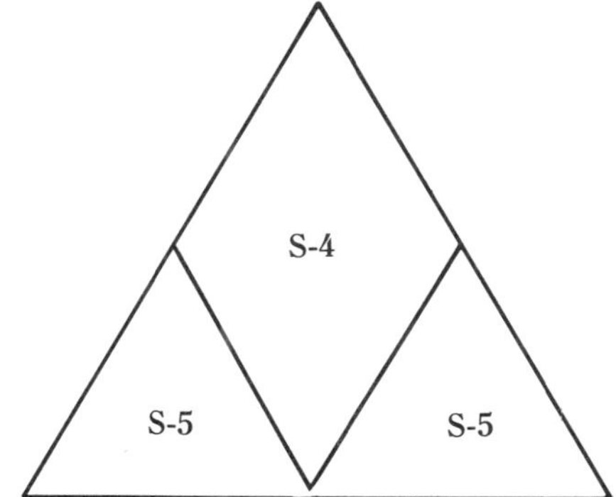

Diagram 2: One-sixth of Six-Point Star

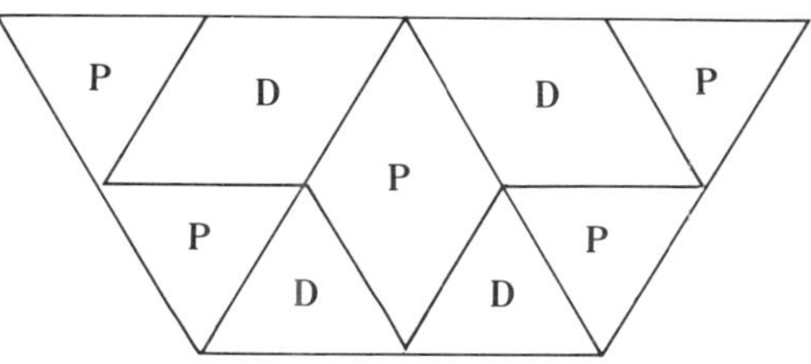

Diagram 3: One-half of Six-Point Star

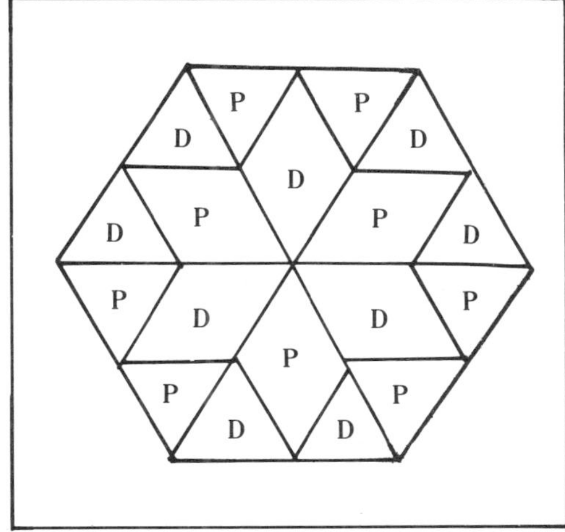

Diagram 4: Six-Point Star

Ship.
S-20: Cut eight light, two print.
S-21: Cut six light, four dark, two print.
Dresden.
S-22: Cut one light.
S-29: Cut ten dark, ten print.
Color Key
L=Light
D=Dark
P=Print

Assembly. *Shoo-fly*: Join small squares (S-3) to form a miniature nine-patch for the center square. Join paired light/print triangles (S-2) to form squares. Join them with the large squares (S-1) and center unit to complete the block in nine -patch fashion, as in Diagram 1.

Six-Point Star: Join two dark triangles (S-5) to the adjacent sides of a print diamond (S-4). See Diagram 2. Repeat for two more units. Make similar units with print triangles and a dark diamond. Join three alternate units for half of the hexagon (see Diagram 3), and three for the other half. Piece in one cross seam to complete the hexagon as in Diagram 4. Turn under the edges of the hexagon ¼″ and appliqué it to a 14½″ background square.

Variable Star: Join paired light/print triangles (S-6) on the short sides to form four units (Diagram 5). Likewise, join four paired dark/print triangle units (Diagram 6). Piece these together to form four squares as in Diagram 7. Join with the large squares (S-1) in nine-patch fashion to complete the block (Diagram 8).

Sunbonnet Sue: Turn under ¼″ seam allowance on all edges of S-7 through S-11, except the top of the skirt, the top of the feet, and the flat end of the hand. Place pieces in center of a 14½″ background square (place bonnet over top of skirt, skirt over top of feet, and flat end of arm over hand). Pin or baste in place and appliqué. See Diagram 9.

Diagram 5: Variable Star

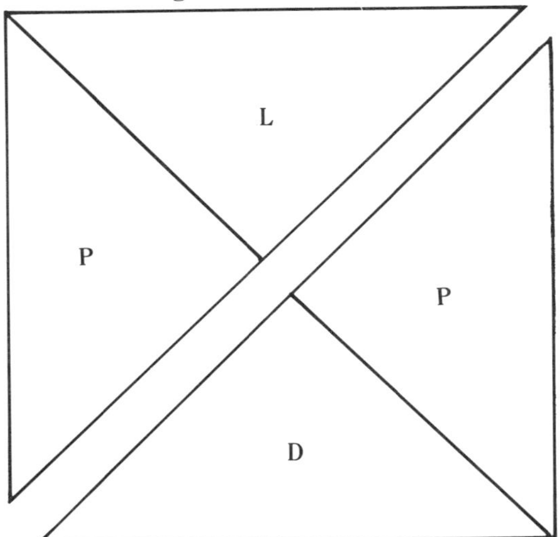

Diagram 6: Variable Star

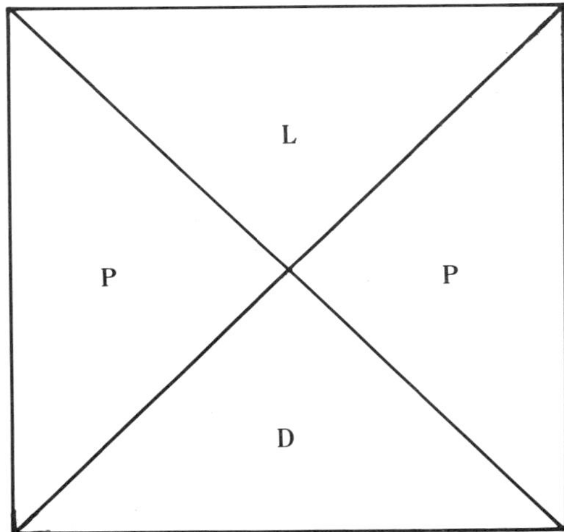

Diagram 7: Variable Star

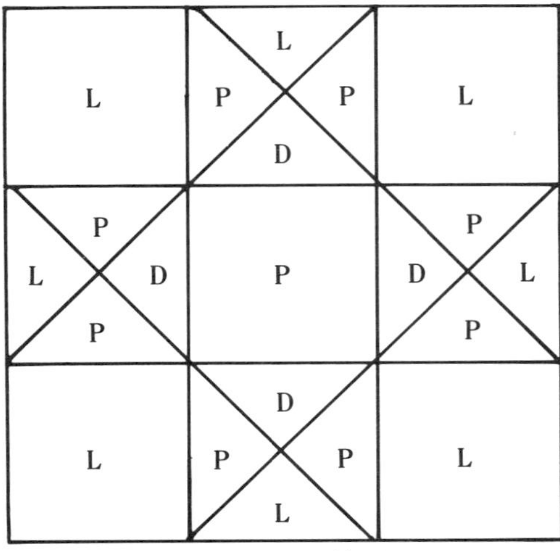

Diagram 8: Variable Star

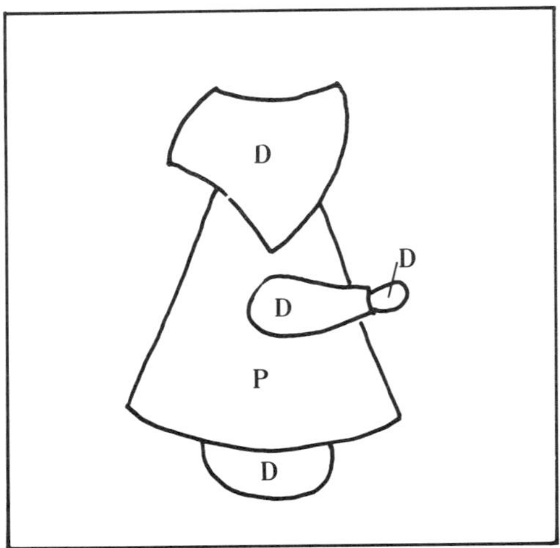

Diagram 9: Sunbonnet Sue

L	P	L	P	L
P	D	P	D	P
L	P	D	P	L
P	D	P	D	P
L	P	L	P	L

Diagram 10: Irish Chain

Irish Chain: Piece five squares (S-12) to make the top row into a rectangular unit (L-P-L-P-L). Do the same with the remaining rows according to Diagram 10. Join units in horizontal seams to form the twenty-five-patch block.

Overall Jim: On pieces S-13 through S-17, turn under ¼″ seam allowances on all edges, except for the top and bottom of the shirt, the flat end of the hands, the ends of the suspenders, and the top edges of the feet. Place pieces in the center of a 14½″ background square (place shirt over hands, suspenders over shirt, pants over suspenders/shirt and feet, and hat over suspenders/shirt). Pin or baste in place according to Diagram 11 and appliqué.

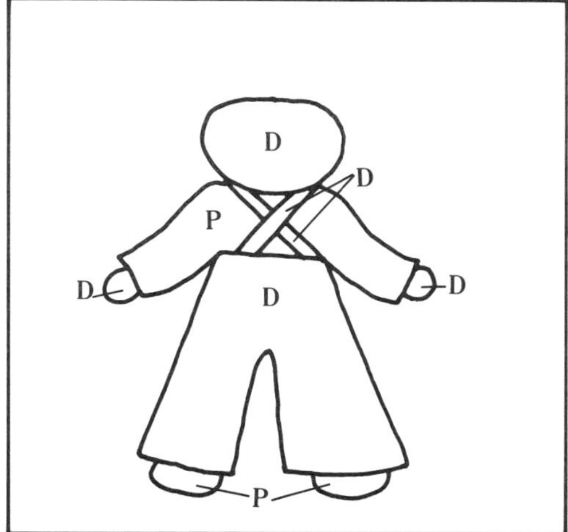

Diagram 11: Overall Jim

Old Maid's Puzzle: Join paired light/print triangles (S-21) on the long side to form six squares, as in Diagram 12. Join two additional light triangles to either side of the print triangle and then add the large dark triangle (S-19), forming a large square, as in Diagram 13. Repeat for a second square. Make two more squares by joining two light squares (S-20) with two pieced squares, as in Diagram 14. Join the four completed units according to Diagram 15 to complete the block.

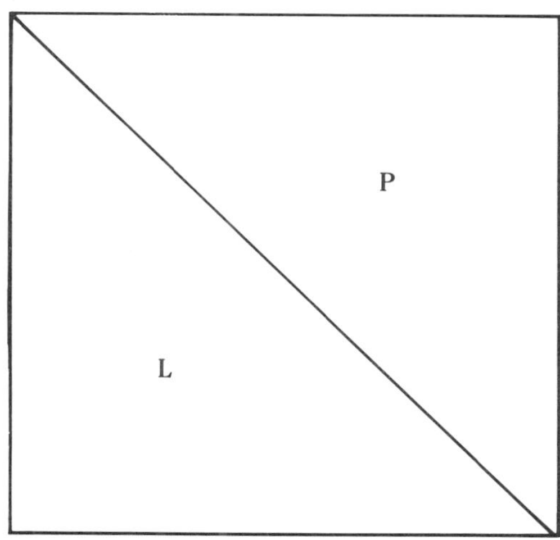

Diagram 12: Old Maid's Puzzle

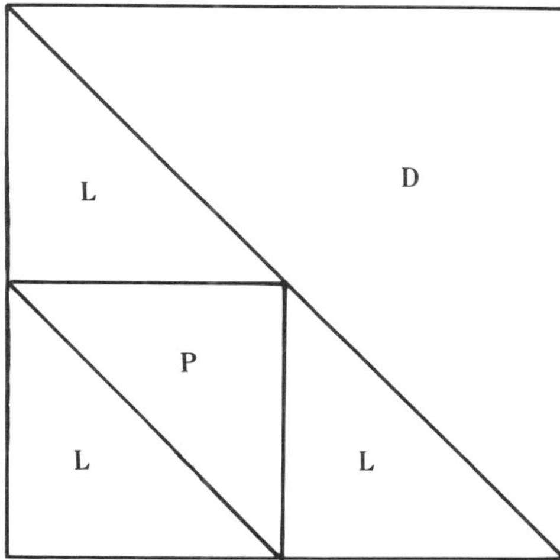

Diagram 13: Old Maid's Puzzle

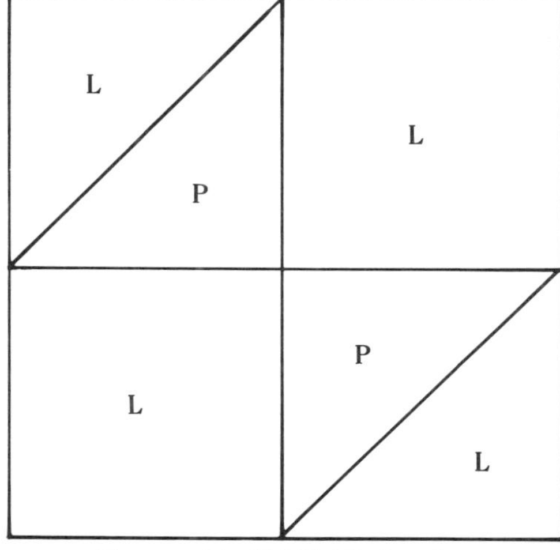

Diagram 14: Old Maid's Puzzle

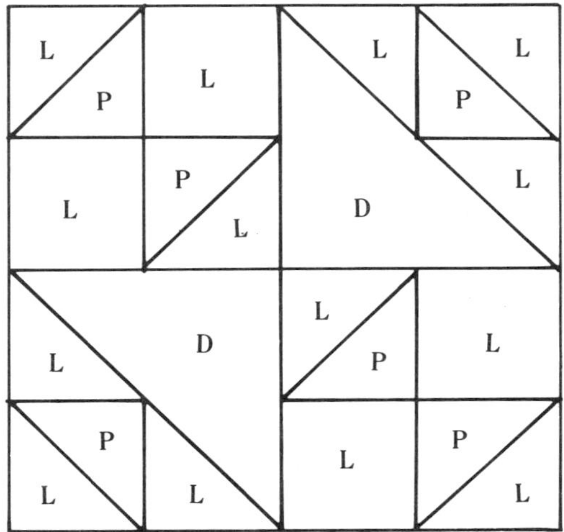

Diagram 15: Old Maid's Puzzle

Dahlia: Turn under ¼″ seam allowances on S-22 through S-24, except for flat end and concave edges of template S-24. Place in the center of a 14½″ background square. Center the circle and place the large petal pieces behind it, fanning out in six equidistant directions, as in Diagram 16. Place the smaller petal pieces beneath and between the larger pieces. Pin or baste in place and then appliqué. *Note*: Excess petal fabric may be trimmed from behind the center circle if it is unsightly.

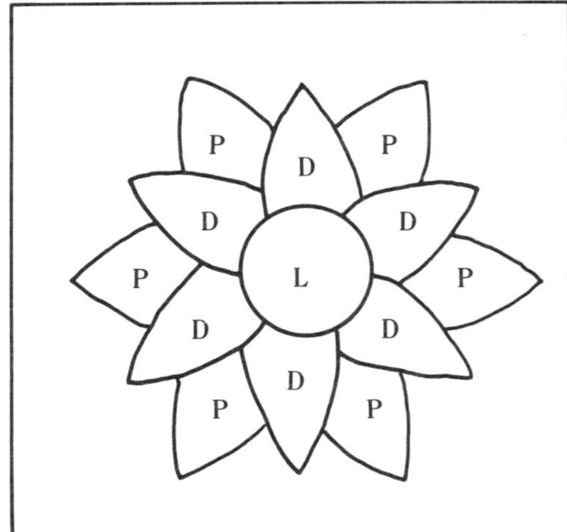

Diagram 16: Dahlia

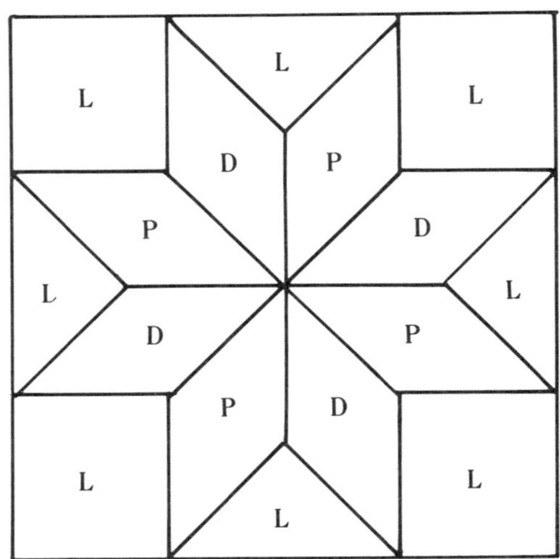

Diagram 17: LeMoyne Star

LeMoyne Star: Join the eight diamonds (S-25) to form a star. This may be done by piecing half of the star and joining it to the other half in one cross seam. Add the four corner squares (S-27) and four side triangles (S-26) in pivot seams to complete the block, as in Diagram 17.

Grandmother's Flower Garden: Join a ring of six dark hexagons (S-28) to the center light hexagon. Then add the outer ring of twelve print hexagons, as in Diagram 18. Turn under ¼″ seam allowances around the outer edge and pin or baste to a 14½″ background square. Appliqué.

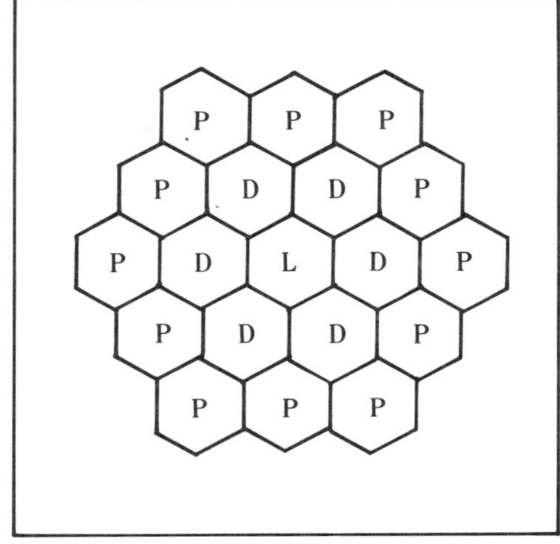

Diagram 18: Grandmother's Flower Garden

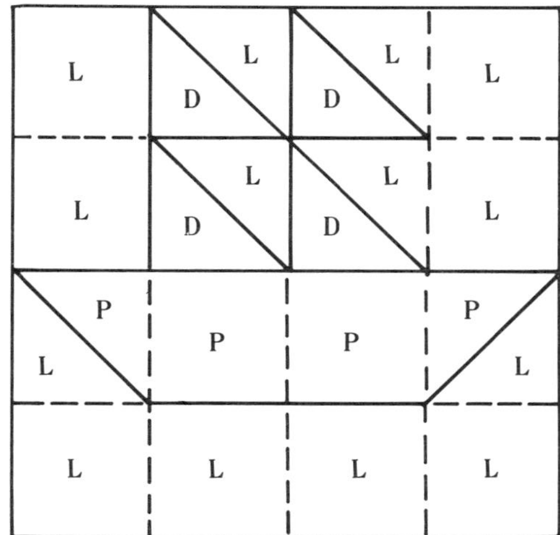

Diagram 19: Ship

Diagram 20: Dresden

Ship: Join paired light/dark triangles (S-21) for the four sails. Join paired light/print triangles (S-21) for ends of hull. Complete the block by joining pieced squares with light or print squares (S-20), as in Diagram 19.

Dresden: Join alternate print and dark wedges (S-29) on long sides to complete a ring. See Diagram 20. Turn under ¼″ on outer (pointed) edges and pin or baste to a 14½″ background square. Turn under edges of light circle (S-22) and place over the center of the ring. Appliqué circle and ring to block.

Diagram 23: Fabric layout for dark pieces

90″

Selvage

3½″ × 54½″ (Cut 5)

Fabric for piecing and appliqué

44″

3½″ × 14½″

(Cut 16)

Selvage

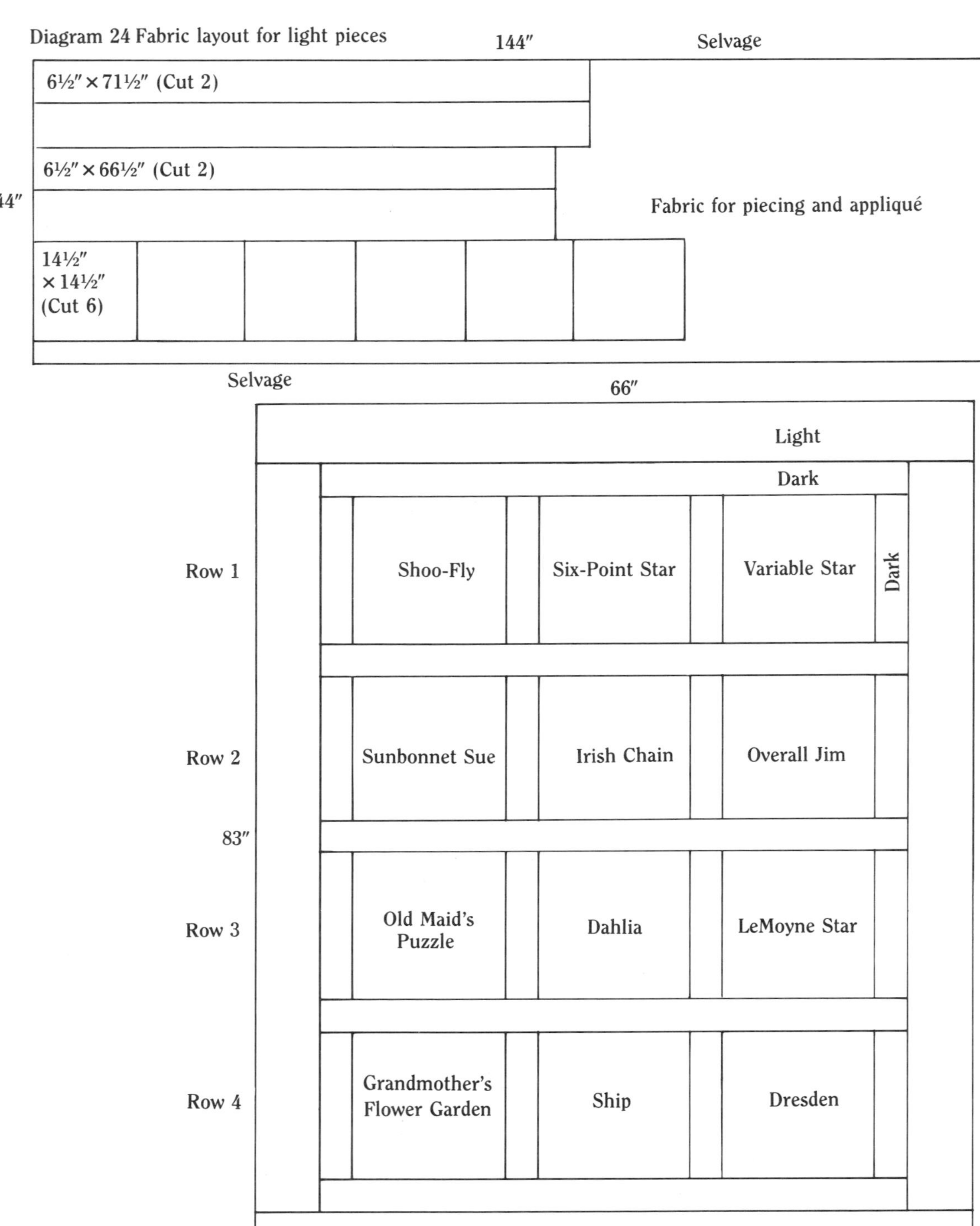

Diagram 22: Sampler layout

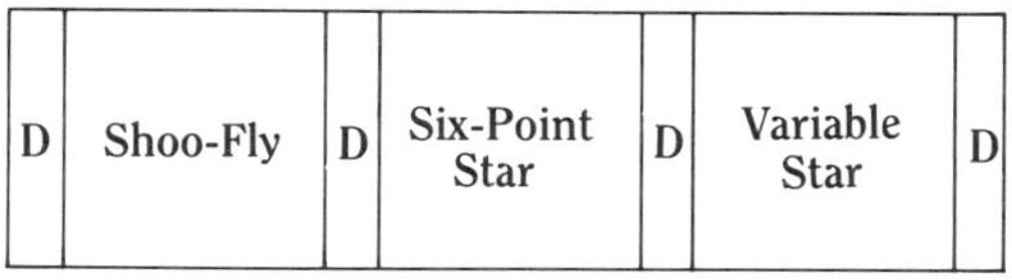

D	Shoo-Fly	D	Six-Point Star	D	Variable Star	D

Diagram 21: Row 1

Latticework and borders. For Row 1, piece three completed blocks and four dark short strips together as in Diagram 21. Make similar units for Rows 2 through 4. Add a long, dark cross-lattice between the rows and at the top and bottom, according to Diagram 22. Add the 6″ side and end borders.

Finishing. With washable marker or soap chip, mark the quilting designs (interlocking rings and ax head) on the borders and latticework. Pin or baste the three layers of the backing, batting, and top together. (See Appendix B: How to Prepare for Quilting.) Quilt close to the seam around all pieces in the twelve blocks. Quilt around each block close to the latticework. Quilt the latticework and border designs. Make and attach the dark binding (see Appendix D: How to Calculate, Make and Apply Continuous Bias Binding).

4

Rainbow Patch

With its mixture of pastel rainbow hues and a soft yellow background, the Rainbow Patch quilt says "summertime." Here is an opportunity to mix and match your assorted pastel scraps or wander through the new summer fabric section of your local store and coordinate new cotton broadcloth solids, fine prints, or tiny ginghams.

Rainbow Patch makes a lovely cradle gift — appropriate for either a boy or girl. It can be used as a summer wall hanging to brighten a nursery. Its smaller size makes it possible to complete this quilt in a reasonable amount of time — hopefully before the baby arrives, or at least before the baby outgrows it.

Piecing can be done by hand or machine. The straightline quilting is not difficult. The border motif is easy to mark and stitch. You will use only one square template, and there are no intricate points to match.

If you are familiar with strip-piecing methods, you could try them on Rainbow Patch. Piece the fabric in long panels, cut them into cross-strips, stagger the rows, and re-assemble. With a few adjustments, the top could be assembled in a matter of hours.

With the addition of an extra border, Rainbow Patch can be adjusted to fit a larger crib or youth bed. An extra 5″ border all around would yield a quilt 45″ × 57″. Use a standard 45″ × 60″ crib batting for this size.

You might want to try border quilting ideas other than the fleur-de-lis used here. Rainbows, stars, balloons, animal cookie cutter shapes, or a diamond grid background are all good possibilities.

Don't say goodbye to quilting in the summertime. Reach for your soft rainbow colors, add a few gentle quilting lines, and you will soon have an attractive wall piece or a lovely baby gift.

Directions

Finished size. 35″ × 47½″.

Materials. Fabric (44″/45″ wide cotton or cotton/polyester blend):

Pink: ¼ yard
Blue: ¼ yard
Light blue: ¼ yard
Green: ¼ yard
Melon: ¼ yard
Cream: ¼ yard
Rose: ¼ yard
Aqua: ⅛ yard
Yellow: 1 yard

Backing: 1½ yards of white
Batting: Crib size (45″ × 60″) bonded polyester

Other supplies. One spool of white quilting thread, sewing thread, 5 yards of white single-fold bias tape for binding, cardboard or plastic for templates, marking pencils or soap chips, pins, scissors, thimble, quilting needles, and iron.

Note. The instructions given here are for a quilt identical to the accompanying photograph. The color aqua is not repeated in the sequence. If you alter the pattern to include a repeat of aqua, increase the aqua yardage to ¼ yard.

Cutting. Cut the yellow border pieces first. Border measurements include seam allowances but do not allow for mitered corners.

Cut two side borders 5½″ × 38″. Cut two end borders 5½″ × 35½″.

Cut the square pieces as follows: For hand piecing, trace the 2½″ square pattern and make a cardboard or plastic template. Place the template on the fabrics and cut 150 squares, adding ¼″ seam all around on the fabric. For machine piecing, include the ¼″ seam allowance on the template, resulting in a 3″ square. Cut the following number of squares:

Pink (P): 18
Blue (B): 19
Light Blue (L): 19
Green (G): 18
Yellow (Y): 18
Melon (M): 18
Cream (C): 18
Rose (R): 17
Aqua (A): 5

Assembly. Join the squares together in rows as given below. For Row 1, piece a pink square to a blue square, etc., ending with a blue square (Row 1: P-B-L-G-Y-M-C-R-P-B). Set Row 1 aside and proceed with Row 2, which begins with a blue square and ends with a light blue square. Continue through Row 15. Each row consists of ten squares.

Row 1: P-B-L-G-Y-M-C-R-P-B
Row 2: B-L-G-Y-M-C-R-P-B-L
Row 3: L-G-Y-M-C-R-P-B-L-G
Row 4: G-Y-M-C-R-P-B-L-G-Y
Row 5: Y-M-C-R-P-B-L-G-Y-M
Row 6: M-C-R-P-B-L-G-Y-M-C
Row 7: C-R-P-B-L-G-Y-M-C-R
Row 8: R-P-B-L-G-Y-M-C-R-P
Row 9: P-B-L-G-Y-M-C-R-P-B
Row 10: B-L-G-Y-M-C-R-P-B-L
Row 11: L-G-Y-M-C-R-P-B-L-A
Row 12: G-Y-M-C-R-P-B-L-A-G
Row 13: Y-M-C-R-P-B-L-A-G-Y
Row 14: M-C-R-P-B-L-A-G-Y-M
Row 15: C-R-P-B-L-A-G-Y-M-C

Press all seams to one side. Press the odd-numbered rows in one direction and even-numbered rows in the opposite direction in order to eliminate bulk at the intersections. When all fifteen rows are complete, join them in horizontal long seams with Row 1 to Row 2, etc., through Row 15 to complete the center of the quilt. See Diagram 1. Press these long seams to one side. Attach the side borders followed by the end borders.

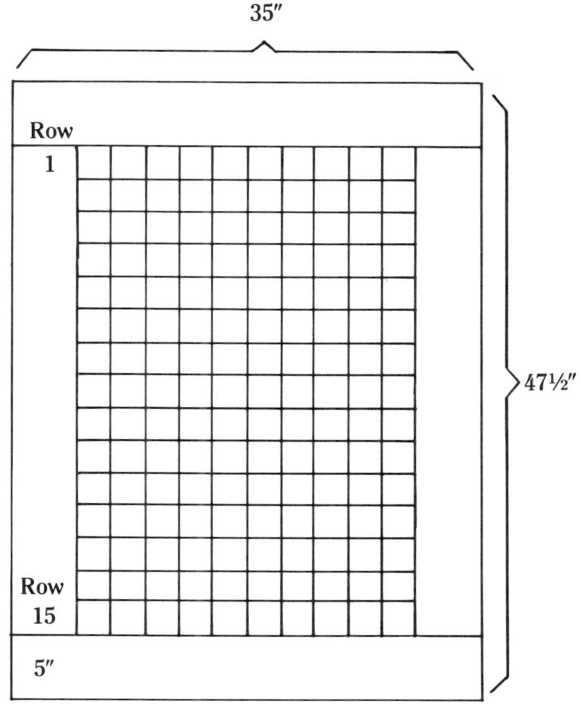

Diagram 1: Rainbow Patch layout

Finishing. Make a cardboard template of the fleur-de-lis design. Carefully mark the border quilting design, centering back-to-back paired templates on sides and ends. See Diagram 2. Mark three pairs on each side border and three pairs on each end border. Mark lightly with a washable marker, soap chip, or dressmaker's pencil. Place the backing fabric right side down. Lay the batting and quilt top over it and baste the three layers together about every 6″-8″. Quilt around all the center squares, close to the seams. Quilt the fleur-de-lis borders. Attach the bias tape binding to the quilt front. Turn the binding to the back and whipstitch to the back of the quilt.

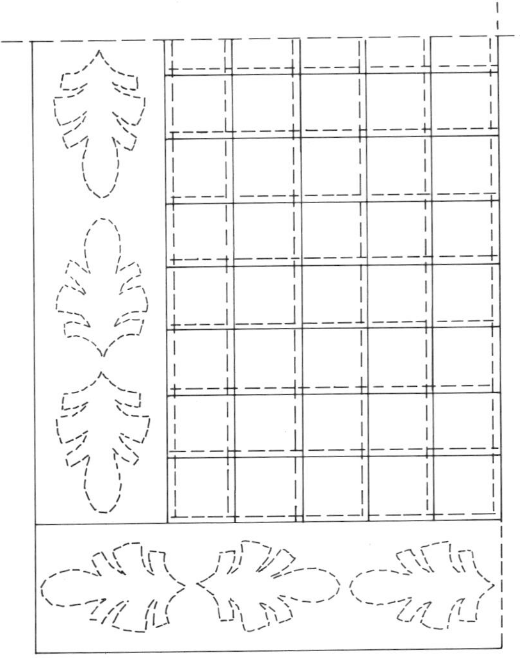

Diagram 2: Rainbow Patch quilting (¼ of quilt)

5

Orange Basket Medallion

Renewed interest in medallion quilts during the past few years has produced many innovative patterns. If you're one of the quiltmakers who has grown tired of the monotony and repetition of block-to-block settings, maybe its time to try a medallion quilt. Breaking out of the block (as I call it) can be a welcome and refreshing stage in your quilting career.

A blend of traditional appliqué and piecing makes Orange Basket Medallion an attractive project. At first glance it may appear to be a complicated pattern. In reality, it is simply a new layout of three old-fashioned patterns: Orange Basket, Trip Around the World, and Jacob's Ladder.

I made the Orange Basket Medallion quilt as a commissioned piece for a church fellowship hall. It was designed to incorporate and reflect the commission for world discipleship. The inscription that accompanies the quilt reads:

> Basket Medallion is created from three traditional American quilt patterns: "Basket of Oranges", "Trip Around the World", and "Jacob's Ladder". The "Basket of Oranges" pattern with its naturalistic fruit and leaves in a patchwork basket is a favorite of several variations of basket and fruit patterns used by American quilters in the past two centuries.
>
> "Trip Around the World" is composed of squares set in a diamond pattern around the central baskets. It symbolizes the path of one traveling around the world.
>
> "Jacob's Ladder" is seen in the outer border, forming a frame for the central patterns. The "staircase" effect of the light floral squares represents the ladder in Jacob's dream.
>
> The quilt is entirely pieced, appliquéd, and quilted by hand. Nine different fabrics are used and there are 1,160 pieces. It measures eighty inches square and is suitable as a wall quilt or for a double bed.
>
> "Basket Medallion" expresses the commission that we go into the world and bring forth fruit.

The medallion setting is quite simple. Other patterns of your choice could be substituted for the basket and ladder sections. Nine-patch patterns other than Jacob's Ladder could be used for the outer borders. The central medallion portion (four 14″ baskets) could be exchanged for other floral appliqué, such as wreaths, pine trees, etc. A different basket pattern, such as the cherry basket or flower basket would be appropriate.

The quilting patterns are based on an orange-cluster motif. This cluster has been adapted to fit the various background shapes and border widths. Quilted orange clusters throughout the design give a continuity from the central medallion across borders and patterns to the outermost brown border.

If trailing vines, oranges, and leaves do not appeal to you, simplify the project with parallel diagonal lines, such as hanging diamonds, on the brown and cream-colored borders. These lines can be marked with masking tape or a straightedge and soap chip.

Orange Basket is also adaptable to smaller projects. The center baskets, set square rather than diagonally, and an additional border would make an ideal wall hanging, about 36″ square. The center baskets with the Trip corners and one brown border would produce a piece about 48″ square.

Orange Basket was a gratifying project for me. Once I started, I was reluctant to put the work down. I was anxious to see my roughly sketched designs come to life in fabric.

Directions

Finished Size. 84″ × 84″

Materials. Fabric (44″/45″ cotton or cotton/polyester blend):

Light print: ¾ yard
Medium print: 1½ yards
Dark print: 2½ yards
Natural: 1⅝ yards
Light orange: ¼ yard
Dark orange: ⅞ yard
Brown: 3 yards
Green: ¼ yard
(Total of 10¾ yards fabric for the quilt top)

Backing: 5¼ yards of good-quality unbleached muslin
Binding: 1 yard of dark brown
Batting: 90″ × 108″ bonded polyester

Other supplies. Cardboard or plastic for templates, light-weight cardboard for pressing templates, iron, thread for appliqué (orange, green, and brown), thread for piecing, two spools of natural-color quilting thread, thimble, pins, quilting needles, scissors, washable fabric markers, thread or pins for basting, hoop or frame for quilting, and a small amount of polyester filling for stuffing the fruit.

Guidelines. The templates for the Orange Basket are coded OB-1 through OB-12. Both piecing and appliqué techniques are used. Seams are ¼″ throughout. There are nine fabrics, twelve templates, and a total of more than 1,100 pieces. The quilt is recommended for quilters with some experience.

Color Key.

LP = Light Print
MP = Medium Print
DP = Dark Print
LO = Light Orange
MO = Medium Orange
DO = Dark Orange
N = Natural
B = Brown
G = Green

Cutting. Wash, dry, and press all fabrics. Make templates from patterns OB-1 through OB-12, being sure to enlarge OB-5 to the measurements indicated on the pattern. Cut the borders from the brown and natural-color fabrics and set these aside (¼″ seams are included in these measurements).

Brown: Cut four 2½″ × 44½″.
Cut four 2½″ × 54½″.
Cut four 6½″ × 84½″ (outer borders).

Natural: Cut four 3½″ × 50½″.

With templates OB-1 through OB-12 cut the number specified below, adding ¼″ seams all around each piece.

OB-1: Cut 20 medium print.
Cut 44 dark print.
Cut 8 natural.
Cut 40 brown.
OB-2: Cut 4 light print.
Cut 64 medium print.
Cut 44 dark print.
Cut 36 natural.
Cut 12 light orange.
Cut 24 dark orange.
OB-3: Cut 4 natural.
OB-4: Cut 8 natural.
OB-5: Cut 4 natural.
OB-6: Cut 4 dark print.
OB-7: Cut 4 dark orange.
OB-8: Cut 8 light orange.
OB-9: Cut 8 dark orange.
OB-10: Cut 28 green.
OB-11: Cut 112 medium print.
Cut 112 dark print.
OB-12: Cut 168 light print.
Cut 56 medium print.
Cut 224 dark print.
Cut 112 dark orange.
(Total of 1,148 pieces).

Assembly. *Basket*: Piece medium and dark print triangles (OB-1) and a medium print square (OB-2) to form the basket, as in Diagram 1. Then join a small natural triangle (OB-1) to the natural rectangle (OB-4) and attach to the side of the basket, as in Diagrams 2 and 3. Repeat for the other side. Attach the base of the basket (OB-3), as in Diagram 3.

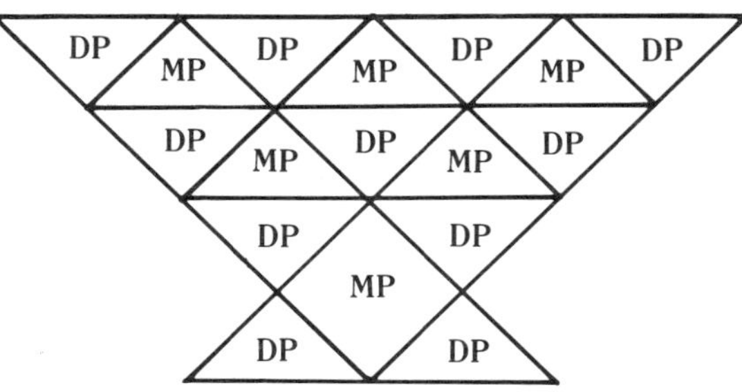

Diagram 1: Orange Basket Medallion

Diagram 2: Orange Basket Medallion

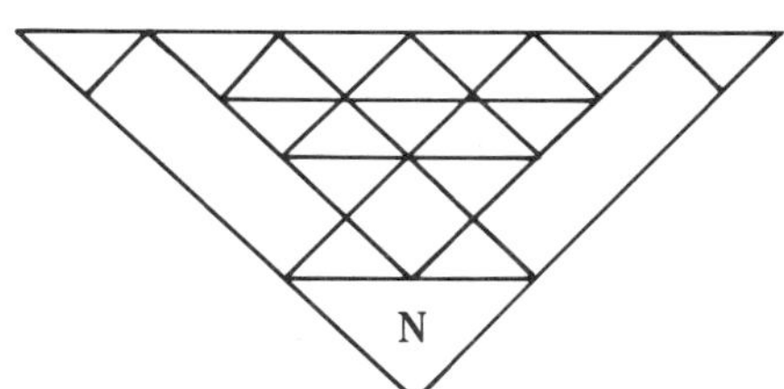

Diagram 3: Orange Basket Medallion

For the appliqué portion, turn under ¼" seam allowances on the curved edges of the fruit, leaves, and handles (OB-6 through OB-10). It is not necessary to turn under the straight sides. Place all appliqué pieces on the large polygon background (OB-5) and pin or baste in place, as shown in Diagram 4. The fruit pieces may be stuffed with a small amount of polyester filling for a raised effect.

Appliqué the fruit, handles, and leaves with matching thread. Join the pieced basket to the appliquéd portion in one crosswise seam. See Diagram 5. Make four basket blocks. Place them with their bases together and the baskets radiating out in four directions. Piece together to complete the center of the quilt.

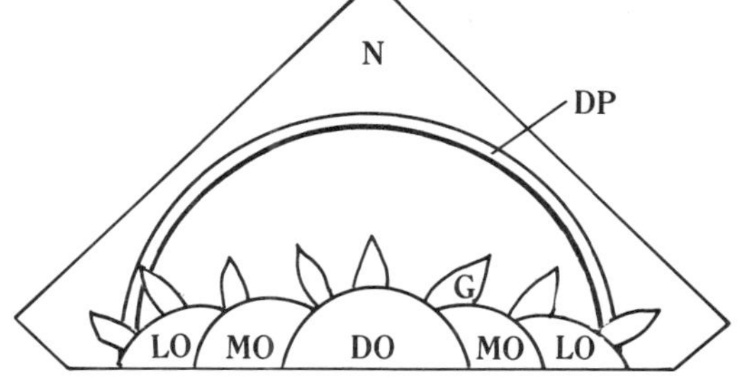

Diagram 4: Orange Basket Medallion

Diagram 5: Orange Basket Medallion

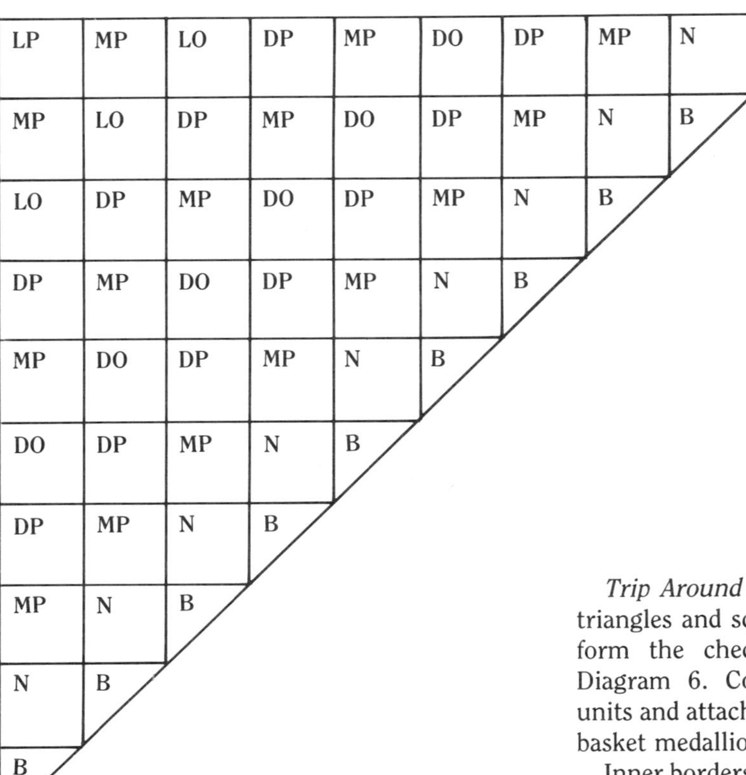

Diagram 6: Trip Around the World

Trip Around the World: Piece together the triangles and squares (OB-1 and OB-2) which form the checkerboard triangle shown in Diagram 6. Complete four such triangular units and attach one to each side of the central basket medallion.

Inner borders: Attach the 2½″ × 44½″ brown borders (all border lengths include seam and miter allowances). Next, attach the 3½″ × 50½″ natural borders. Last, attach the 2½″ × 54½″ brown borders. See Diagram 8 for borders.

Jacob's Ladder border: Piece four small squares (OB-12) of light print and dark print fabric to form Unit A. Make eighty-four such units. Piece similar squares of dark orange, medium print, and dark print to form Unit B, as illustrated. Make fifty-six such units. Join the dark and medium print triangles (OB-11) along the long side to make Unit C, as illustrated. Make 112 of Unit C. Then piece A, B, and C as shown in Diagram 7 to form twenty-eight completed 9″ blocks. Piece a row of six Jacob's Ladder blocks to create a stairstep effect and attach to the side of the quilt. See Diagram 8 and the quilt photograph. Repeat for the other side. Likewise, join eight blocks and attach to the bottom of the quilt. Repeat for the top of the quilt.

Outer Borders: Attach the 6½″ × 84½″ brown borders to all sides of the quilt (measurement includes allowance for mitering).

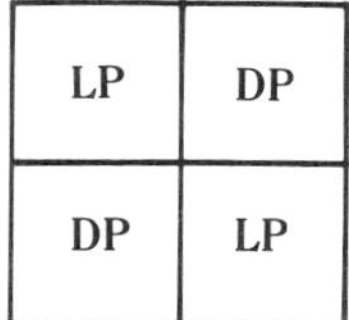

Unit A (make 84)

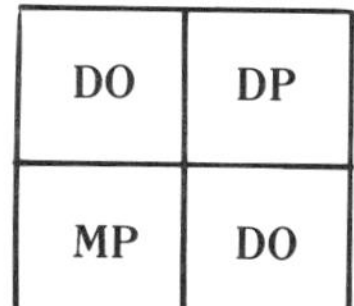

Unit B (make 56)

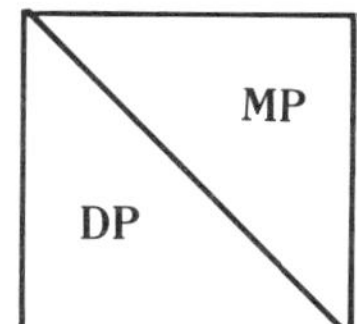

Unit C (make 112)

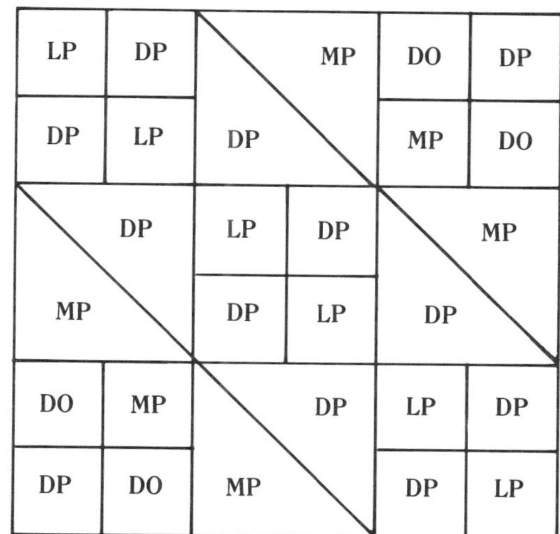

Diagram 7: Jacob's Ladder (make 28)

Quilting. Sandwich the completed top, batting, and back together (see Appendix B: How to Prepare for Quilting). With a washable marking pencil, mark the quilt designs. Quilt with natural-color quilting thread.

In the basket blocks, mark a wreath of oranges in the center of the quilt, orange clusters between the baskets, and trailing orange clusters outside the basket handles. Quilt the marked designs, plus several rows of shadow quilting inside the handles, and in the ditch around all pieces.

In the Trip Around the World sections, quilt in the ditch close to the seams around all squares and triangles.

On the inner and outer borders, quilt trailing orange clusters.

In the Jacob's Ladder blocks, quilt in the ditch around all triangles and squares.

Finishing. Remove all bastings and finish the edges with binding made from the one-yard piece of dark brown fabric. (See Appendix D: How to Calculate, Make, and Apply Continuous Bias Binding.)

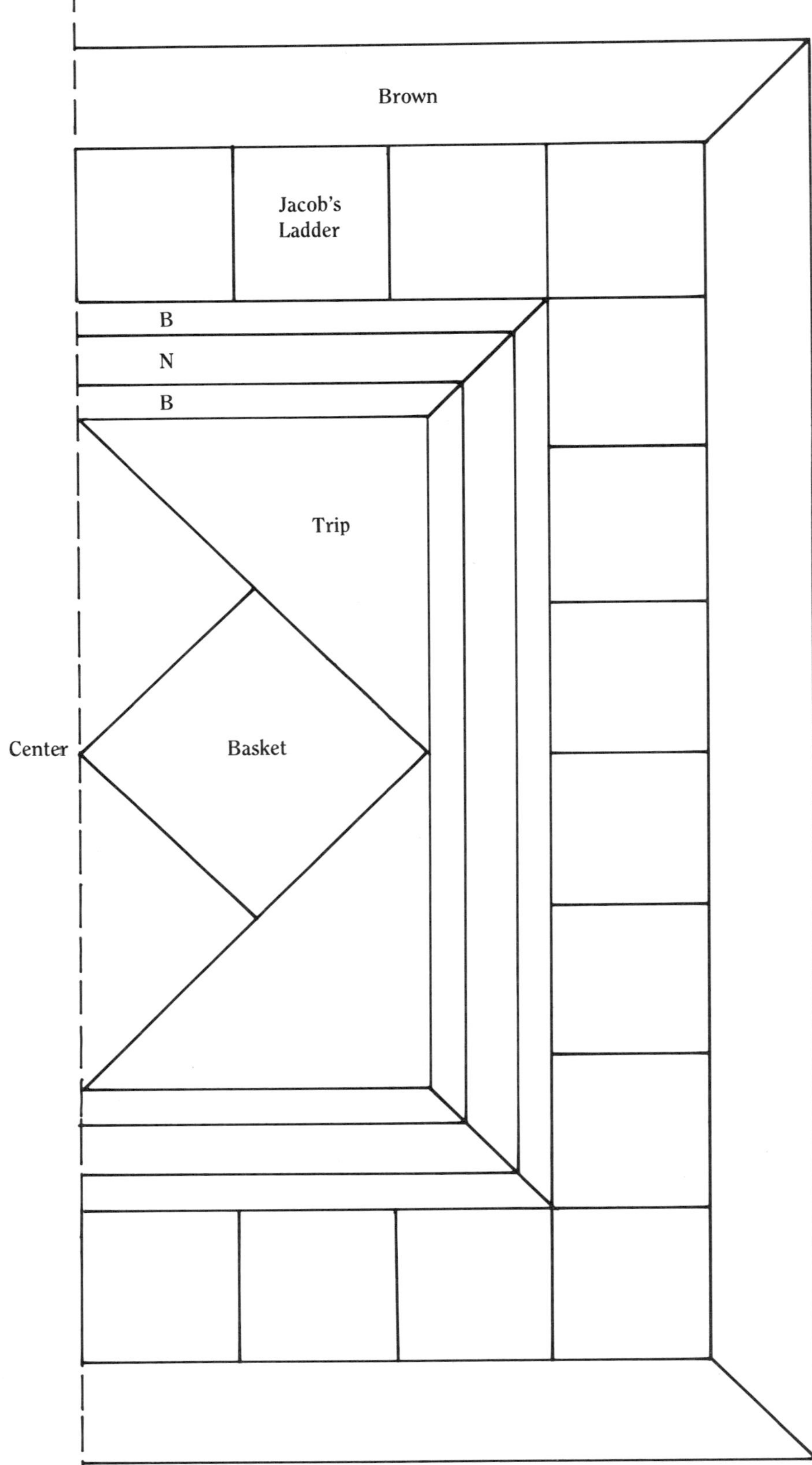

Diagram 8: Orange Basket Medallion layout (½ of quilt)

Orange Basket Medallion. 84″ × 84″. Piecing, appliqué, and quilting skills are all necessary for this detailed quilt.

Triangles. 70″ × 80″. Easy to sew from fabric scraps.

Rainbow Patch. 35″ × 47½″. Simple to piece, the quilt's beauty is in the choice of colors and quilting motif.

Spring. 35″ × 45″. Appropriate for beginners as well as experienced quilters.

Spring. Detail of birdhouse, shamrock, and umbrella quilting designs.

Spring. Rows of diagonal quilting on the borders meet the corners and centers of the fabric strips.

Sampler. 66″ × 83″. An excellent project for practice in piecing and appliqué.

Sampler. Detail of Old Maid's Puzzle block.

Sampler. Interlocking rings are quilted with a contrasting color of thread.

Holiday. 37″ × 47″. Similar to the Spring quilt, rows of alternating colors are enhanced by quilted designs.

6

Holiday

Many families have a traditional quilt that they display or use only during the holiday season. Often it is a quilt of festive reds and greens that is used at the foot of the bed or as a decorative greeting in the entryway of a home.

Knowing that a holiday quilt might be used for only a few weeks of the year, many quilters cannot justify spending a lot of time in its construction. A sensible alternative is a wall hanging that can be hung during the holidays and rotated with other seasonal pieces, such as Spring and Rainbow Patch wall hangings that are also featured in this book.

The Holiday quilt is constructed in the same basic fashion as Spring, with no template, piecing, or appliqué required. The modified whole-cloth panels can be cut and assembled by machine in a matter of hours. The major time requirement is in the hand-quilted designs. This is the part that makes the piece come to life.

Several of the quilted designs are based on cookie-cutter shapes. Check among your cookie cutters or an antique collection for shapes to adapt into quilting designs. The Holiday instructions include patterns for a wreath, candle, reindeer, star, stocking, tree, and gingerbread person. Other possibilities include an angel, a trumpet, a rocking horse, a poinsettia, or a candy cane.

A mixture of deep reds and greens is used on the seven center panels. These are accented with a neutral tan border, binding, and ribbon bows. Although you may confine your color selection to one green and one red, the blending of several deep reds and forest greens will enrich the quilt surface. You may find colors with the richness of velvet and the smoothness of satin to include in your quilt.

Don't wait until November or December to start on your holiday project. Beginning in early fall will assure completion before your first holiday guests arrive.

Directions

Finished Size. 37″ × 47″.

Materials. Fabric (44″/45″ wide cotton or cotton/polyester blend):

- Two deep forest green solids: 1/4 yard of each
- Another deep solid green: 5/8 yard (for a center panel and borders)
- Three deep red solids: 1/4 yard of each
- Another deep red solid: 5/8 yard (for a center panel and borders)
- Deep tan solid: 1 1/8 yards (for borders and binding)

Backing: 1 1/2 yards unbleached muslin

Batting: Bonded polyester at least 40″ × 50″ (a standard crib batt is 45″ × 60″).

Other Supplies. 4 1/2 yards deep tan double-faced 1/8″ wide satin ribbon, sewing machine thread, scissors, one spool of deep tan or natural-color quilting thread, frame or hoop for quilting, washable marking pencil or soap chip, ruler, cardboard or plastic for quilting templates, sewing machine, quilting needles, thimble, pins, thread for basting, iron, and (optional) rotary cutter and mat.

Cutting. Seam allowances are included on all border and panel measurements. However, the measurements do not include enough for mitered corners. Add about 6″ to the length of each border measurement if you wish to miter the corners. All borders and panels must be cut on the crosswise of the fabric. (There will not be enough fabric in the recommended yardage to cut along the lengthwise grain.) Cut the following, being sure to cut borders first.

Deep tan: Cut two side borders 2½" × 35½".
Cut two end borders 2½" × 29½".
Red (from ⅝ yard piece):
Cut two side borders 2½" × 39½".
Cut two end borders 2½" × 33½".
Cut one panel 5½" × 25½".
Green (from ⅝ yard piece):
Cut two side borders 2½" × 43½".
Cut two end borders 2½" × 37½".
Cut one panel 5½" × 25½".

From each of the other five green and red fabrics, cut a panel 5½" × 25½" (¼" seams included).

Assembly. Pin and then stitch the long sides of each panel (with right sides together) in ¼" seams, alternating red and green panels (see Diagram 1). Press the seams to one side. Join the borders to the center panels, beginning with the inner (tan) border. For each border, attach the sides first, then the ends. See Diagram 1. Press all seams toward the outside.

Quilting. Make templates of the seven cookie-cutter shapes (wreath, candle, reindeer, star, stocking, tree, and gingerbread person). Divide each panel into five 5" squares, marking lightly with a soap chip or washable marker.

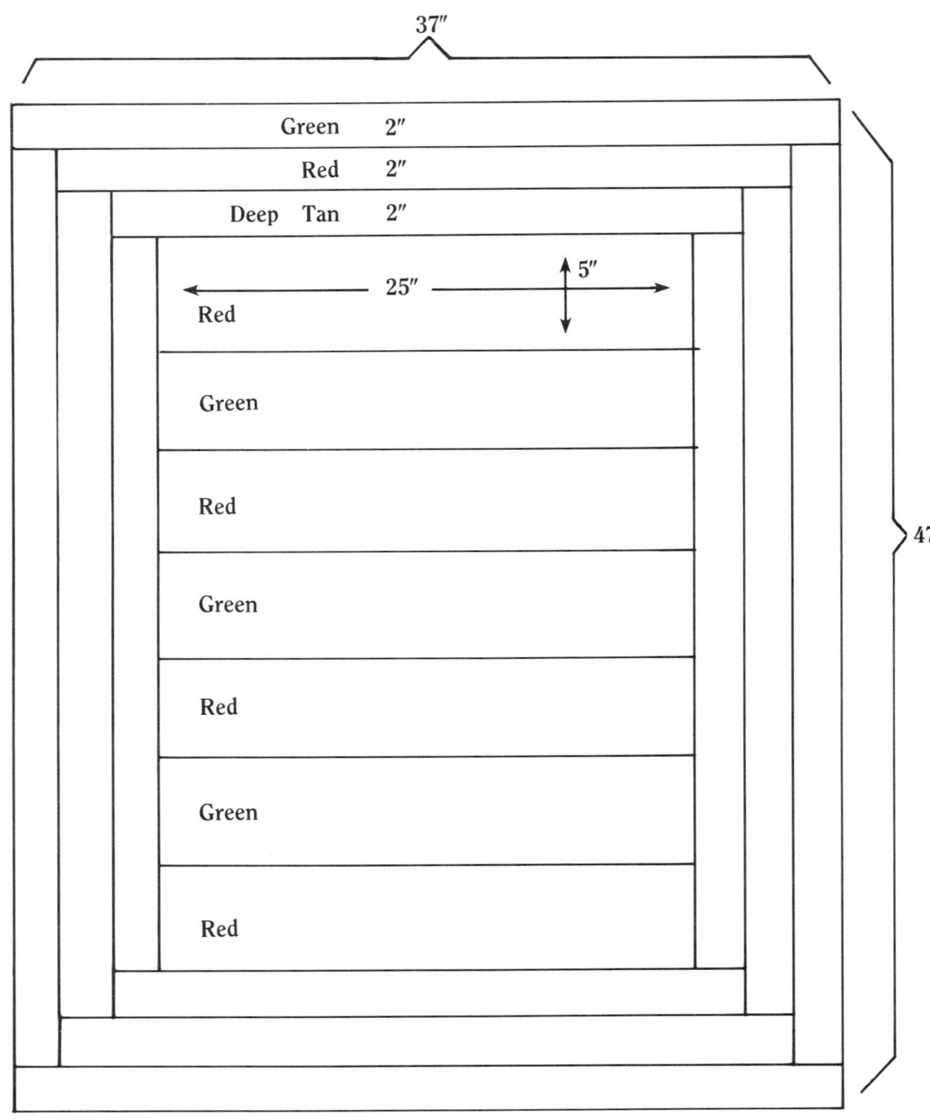

Diagram 1: Holiday

Center the quilting design in each square and mark lightly, filling in any details such as the eyes or legs of the reindeer or lines in the star. Mark five designs in each panel.

Cut a piece of unbleached muslin about 39″ × 49″ for the back of the quilt. Place this right side down on a flat surface and layer the batting and the quilt top (right side up) over it. Pin and carefully baste the three layers (see Appendix B: How to Prepare for Quilting). Using a frame or hoop, quilt the central designs, the crosswise seams, and across the three borders as shown in Diagram 2. Diagonal lines are about 2½″ apart. Remove basting.

Finishing. From the remaining deep tan fabric, cut bias strips 3″ wide and piece them to a sufficient length to border the quilt (about 5 yards). Fold the bias in half lengthwise with the wrong sides together. Pin the binding to the quilt top, with raw edges flush. Stitch a ¼″ seam through all layers. Turn the folded edge of the binding to the quilt back and whipstitch it to the back. From the ⅛″ double-faced satin ribbon, cut twenty 7″ lengths. Fold them into bows (see Diagram 3) and tack them to each of the following quilt designs: wreath, reindeer, stocking, and gingerbread person.

Diagram 3: Holiday

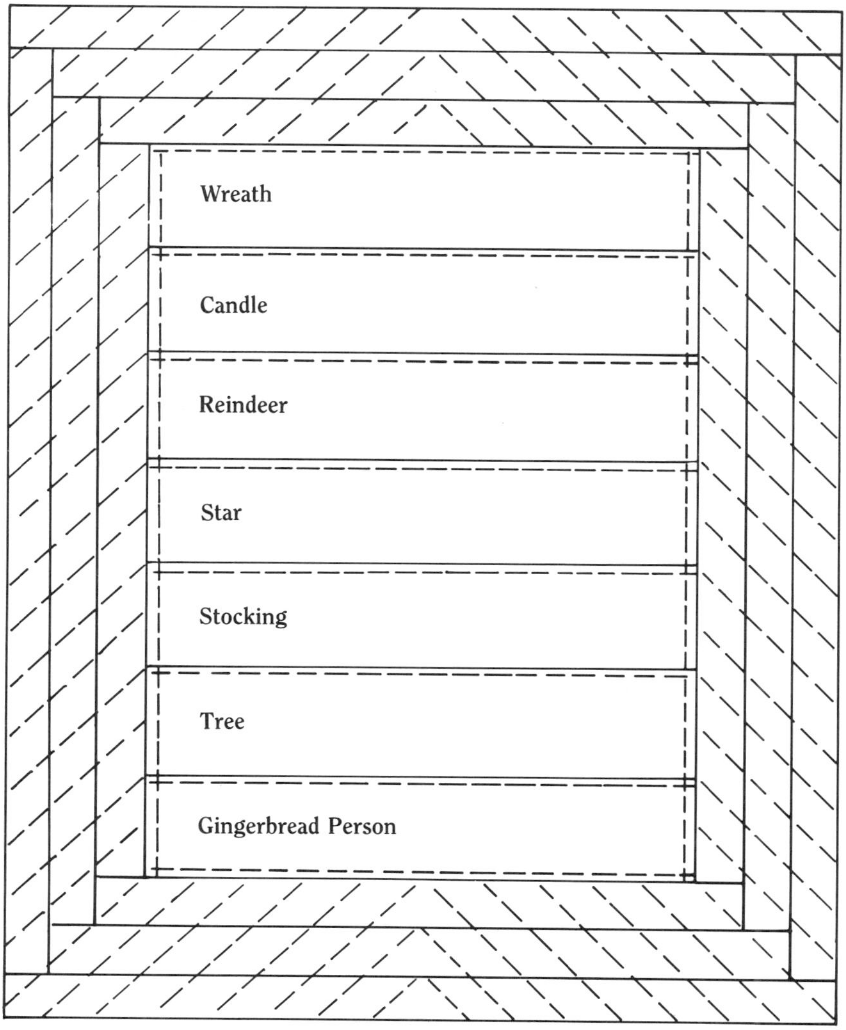

Wreath

Candle

Reindeer

Star

Stocking

Tree

Gingerbread Person

Diagram 2: Holiday

Appendix A
Ten Tips for Precision Cutting and Hand-Piecing

1. Trace or draft the pattern pieces precisely, using a sharp pencil. Use plastic or stiff cardboard for the templates. Do not include seam allowances on the templates. Cut templates along the inside of the traced or drafted lines.

2. Mark the grain lines on the template with an arrow. Generally, place grain lines on edges that will fall on the outside of an assembled unit or block.

3. Write the pattern name, the number to be cut, your name or initials, and the words "add ¼″ seam" on each template.

4. Place the template on the wrong side of pre-washed, pressed fabric, allowing for seams all around. Hold the template securely with one hand and mark the corner points with the point of the pencil. Then draw lines to join the dots, moving from the corner point to the center side, then from the other corner to the center side. This will help prevent distortion of the points.

5. To join the pieces, match and pin the points at both ends of a seam. Pin along the seam with crosswise pins to make sure that the seams are lined up. Turn over the pieces to check the back side. For a short seam of less than 3″, one crosswise pin and the two end pins will be sufficient. For longer seams, add more crosswise pins.

6. Using a fine needle (Betweens #7 through #10) and a strand of thread no longer than 18″, begin sewing at the marked point on one end of the seam. Take a small stitch through both pieces, leaving a short tail. Take another stitch on top of it to secure the thread. Continue with small running stitches, taking two or three at a time. Take an occasional backstitch to reinforce the seam.

7. End the seam with a stitch at the marked point at the end of the seamline. Take a backstitch directly on top of the last stitch to secure it. Cut the thread, leaving a short tail.

8. Continue joining pieces to complete a unit or block. Finger-press the seams as you cross them, always leaving the seams free. Do not sew the seams down. Instead, slip the needle through the seam allowances to continue sewing. This will allow you the freedom you need to press the finished block.

9. When an entire unit or block has been pieced, you may steam-press it. For best results, press over a terry cloth towel. Beginning on the wrong side, press all seams to one side, using your best judgment and common sense to minimize the bulk and avoid "shadowing" of darker fabrics behind the lighter ones. It should not be necessary (and it is not advisable) to cut, clip, or trim any seam allowances, unless they cause an unsightly shadow behind a lighter fabric.

10. Turn the block over and steam-press it on the right side. Then hold it up, sigh, and smile.

Appendix B
How to Prepare for Quilting

Many quilters do not recognize the importance of the steps taken after they finish a quilt top and before they begin quilting. Proper preparation of the backing, batting, and the finished top are crucial to an outstanding finished product. Don't skip these steps. Even the most perfectly executed quilt stitches won't make up for errors made in preparation of the three layers.

Here are some useful pointers, including special advice for the use of smooth and carpeted surfaces in laying and stretching your quilt.

1. Piece the quilt backing. Make it about 2″ to 3″ larger than the quilt top on all sides in order to avoid shortages. It's better to be safe with an ample backing than to have to trim some of your quilt top to accommodate a skimpy back.

2. Last Chance Pressing: Carefully steam-press the quilt top, wrong side first, in order to press seams uniformly. Use a generous amount of steam. Then turn the top right side up and press again, if necessary. Remember that pressing is an up/down motion, not back and forth as in ironing. Too much lateral movement will distort your quilt top. Press the quilt backing as well.

3. Joining the three layers on a carpeted surface: (The steps that follow are easier to do with help from a partner. Go get that helper now.)

A. Lay the pressed backing right side down. Gently stretch and pin the edges to the floor with T-pins, placing them about a foot apart and set at an angle away from the quilt center. Pull the back taut enough to remove all wrinkles.

B. Lay the batting over the back. The batting need not be as large as the backing, but it should be at least an inch larger than the quilt top on all sides. Do not stretch the batt.

C. Lay the pressed quilt top, right side up over the batting. Smooth the top until it's free of wrinkles. Be sure that the batting and backing are exposed on all four sides. Hold the three layers taut with one hand and transfer the T-pins from the bottom layer to the quilt top and through all three layers.

D. Start at one end of the quilt and reach underneath the layers with one hand. With the other hand on top, pin (with regular stick pins) through all three layers, being careful not to catch them in the carpet (the hand underneath will guide you). Pin along the edge and in as far as the arms can reach, with pins about every 12″ or so. Your partner can work from the other end of the quilt.

E. Next, transfer the T-pins toward the center along the edge of the unsecured area. Fold up the pinned area and repeat Step D until you reach the center (or your partner).

F. Remove all T-pins and transfer the quilt to a table. Thread-baste in diagonal and crisscross lines every few inches.**

G. Thus prepared, the piece is ready for lap, hoop, or frame quilting.

4. Joining the three layers on a smooth surface (floor or tables):

This process is more efficient than the one done on a carpeted surface. First read the above directions, then recruit your helper and follow these steps.

A. Stretch the backing as above, and fasten it to the smooth surface with masking tape.

B. Layer the batt and quilt top over the backing. Stretch gently to remove fullness, and secure the three layers to the floor (or table) with additional masking tape.

C. Beginning near the center, pin or thread-baste through all layers. For pin-basting, use small rustproof safety pins and pin through all layers, about every 6″ to 8″, and along the outer edges. For thread-basting, you will have to reach long distances or use a "hands and knees" method. Baste in diagonal and crisscross lines every few inches.**

**The amount of basting (or number of safety pins) depends on what method of quilting you plan to use. For quilting on a frame (large free-standing or roller frame), where you have good control over the tension of the three layers, basting does not have to be as dense. Basting every 8″ to 10″ will suffice. Indeed, if your frame stretches the quilt evenly, you may not need any basting at all. For quilting with a hoop, I suggest adding more basting, approximately every 6 ″ to 8″. For lap or table quilting, even more basting is needed. I recommend every 3″ to 4″.

In all cases, be sure to baste along the edge of the quilt top, through all three layers. I recommend a line of basting within ¼″ of the edge. This will secure the edges and minimize the stretching and distortion from handling during the quilting and binding processes. Ideally, this line of basting can stay in the quilt forever. If it is within the outer ¼″ seam allowance, it will be covered by the binding.

Appendix C
How to Create Your Own Quilting Designs

Some of the most impressive quilting designs are also the most elementary. Complication and intricacy are not essential for effective designs. A simple design can be arranged and adapted into useful quilting patterns.

In the following examples I have listed and diagrammed guidelines for making original quilting designs. These steps are easy to follow, and the designs are not difficult. I have used similar procedures to make many of my own quilting designs. For instance, the four quilting designs for Orange Basket Medallion are based on a simple orange cluster motif arranged to fit various shaped background and border areas.

Some of the Orange Basket designs are outlined below. Read through the procedures and examples. Then start over with a pencil, an eraser, and a clean piece of paper, and try making your own designs. The possibilities are infinite.

1. Define and measure the background areas and borders that require and will accommodate a quilted design.

Example: For the central basket area, I selected three areas for quilting — the center muslin square (made of four pieced triangles from the bases of the baskets), the arrow-shaped muslin areas between the baskets, and the muslin area on the outside of the basket handles. I also selected two borders that were wide enough to accommodate a quilting design — the inner muslin border and the outer dark brown border.

2. Make a paper pattern of each of the background or border areas. Lightly pencil in ¼″ clearance lines around the space (to avoid quilting lines through bulky seam areas). Then lightly mark grid lines that bisect or divide the space into smaller workable units.

Example: For the center square, I cut a 5⅝″ square of paper. I marked the ¼″ clearance lines and an X to divide it into four equal triangles (see Diagram 1).

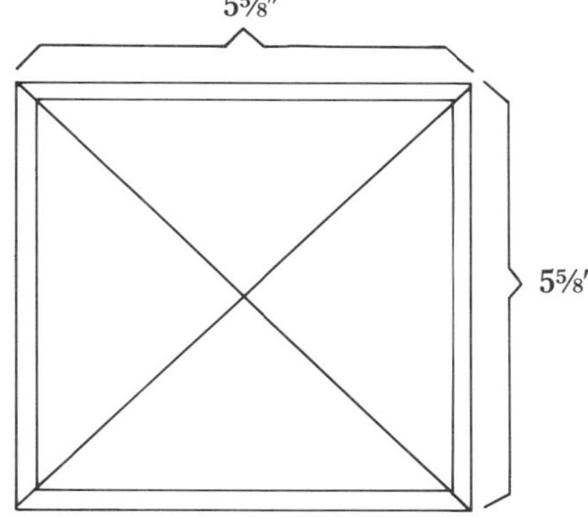

Diagram 1 (not to scale)

3. Select a motif that complements the pattern of the quilt top. This may be a pieced or appliquéd shape or a design from within one of the fabrics. Draw the motif and make a plastic template.

Example: For the Orange Basket quilt I chose an orange-leaf motif. I drew a small cluster of two oranges and two leaves and made a plastic template (see Diagram 2).

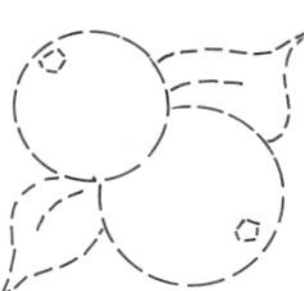

Diagram 2

4. Vary the size of other motifs that might be useful in border and background areas. Draw the motif and make the template.

Example: For Orange Basket I made a second larger cluster of three oranges and three leaves, as in Diagram 3.

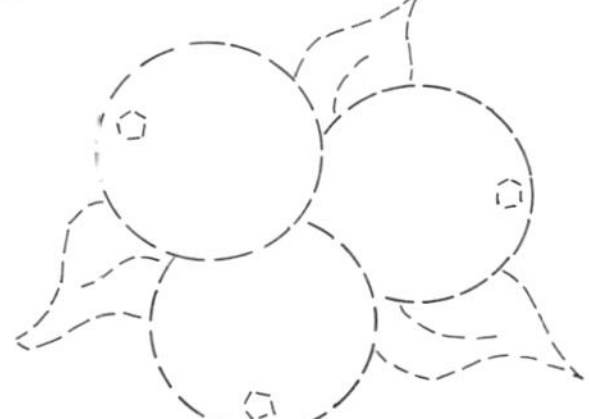

Diagram 3

5. Place the design motif template on the gridded paper areas, experimenting to find comfortable spacing and a pleasing design. Try several placement variations by turning or reversing the template, moving from corners to sides, etc.

Example: For the center of Orange Basket, I used the small orange cluster. I centered one motif on each triangular area, with the larger orange toward the outside of the square (see Diagram 4).

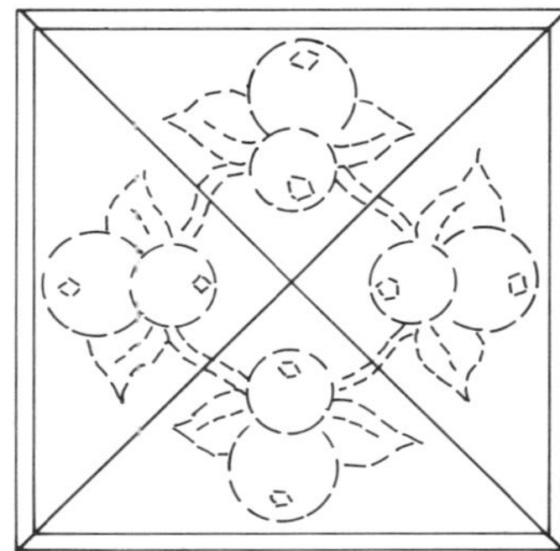

Diagram 4 (not to scale)

6. Add any details that will enhance the quilted design. Then erase all grid and clearance lines.

Example: To complete the center square of Orange Basket, I added blossom ends on the oranges and joined the orange clusters with a curved vine, giving the effect of a wreath or garland.

I followed similar steps to make the quilting design for the arrow-shaped areas between the baskets (see Diagram 5).

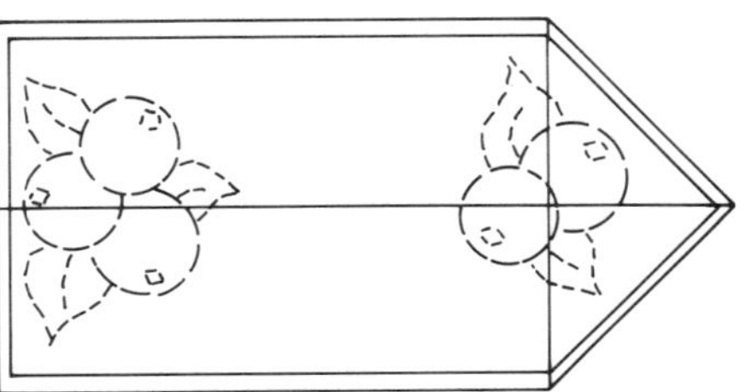

Diagram 5 (not to scale)

First I measured and drew the ¼″ clearance lines and a vertical bisecting line. Because the width varies from one end to the other, use of both the small and large orange clusters is appropriate. I placed a small one near the narrow pointed end and a larger cluster at the opposite wider end. The remaining space between was adequate for another small motif, which I added.

To complete the design, I added extra leaves on the small clusters, blossom ends on the oranges, and a trailing vine, which continues on to join the quilted design around the basket handles (see Diagram 6).

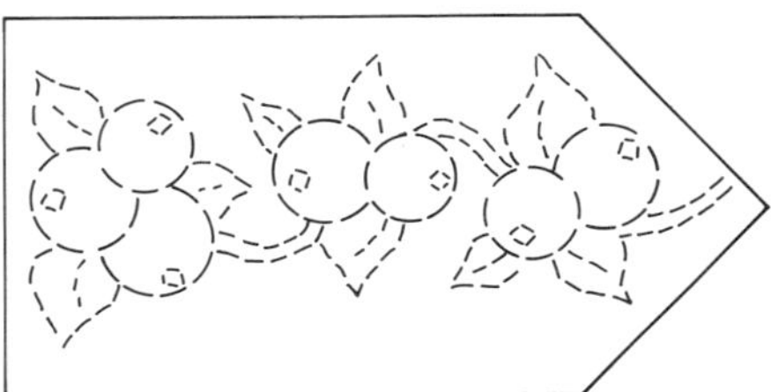

Diagram 6 (not to scale)

The quilting designs for the area around the basket handles and the two borders (muslin and outer dark brown) were made in a similar fashion. I used a combination of small and large clusters. In the borders I placed a large cluster in each corner and alternated it with a small cluster, with trailing vines along the way. For the basket handle area I placed one large cluster at the top of each handle and a large/small combination at each side corner, joined by trailing vines. See the Orange Basket Medallion full-sized quilting designs for placement and details.

Appendix D
How to Calculate, Make and Apply Continuous Bias Binding

Many quilt books give instructions on how to make continuous bias for binding. They usually give diagrams and proclaim the advantages of a certain type of binding, but fail to tell you how to calculate the amount of fabric you need to make binding for your quilt. They omit the secret for avoiding shortages or excesses of binding.

Here is a method to figure the amount of fabric required for continuous bias binding. I have also included steps for making and attaching the binding.

A. How to calculate the amount

1. Measure the distance around the quilt in inches (2 Lengths + 2 Widths = Distance).
2. Add 25″ to allow for corners and miters.
3. Multiply this number by the width the bias is to be *cut*. For a finished double binding about ½″ wide (which is what I use and recommend), you'd cut the bias strips 3″ wide. So multiply by 3.
4. Find the square root of this number. (Don't panic! A pocket calculator will do the job just fine.)
5. Round this number up to the next largest whole number and add 2″ to allow for seams and error. Cut or piece a square of fabric this size.

Example: Quilt size is 81″ × 96″

81 + 81 + 96 + 96 = 354″

354 + 25 = 379″

379 × 3 = 1137 square inches

The square root of 1,137 is 33.7″

Round up to 34 and add 2″, equalling 36″. For this quilt, you should buy a yard of fabric or make a pieced square 36″ × 36″.

B. How to make the bias

1. Make a true square of fabric (as calculated above). This may be an intact or pieced square.
2. Mark a diagonal line along the bias from corner to corner. Cut along this line. There will be two triangles the same size. See Diagram 1.

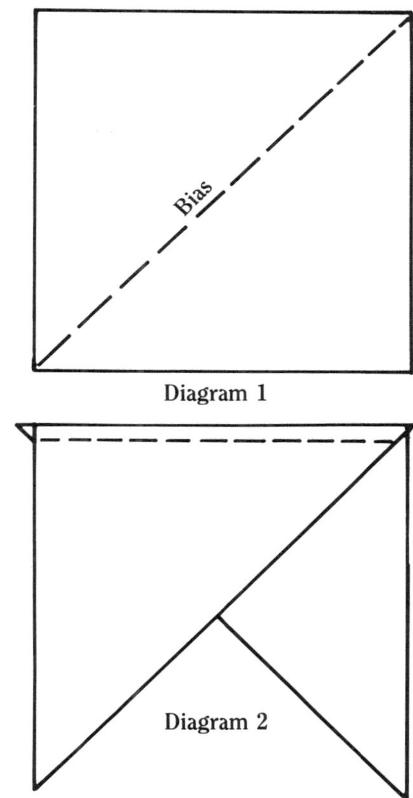

Diagram 1

Diagram 2

3. Place the short sides of the triangles, right sides together, as in Diagram 2, and join in a ¼″ seam.

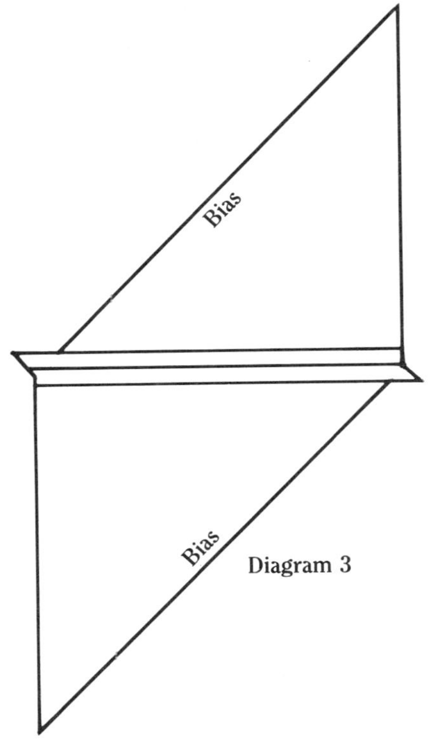

Diagram 3

4. Press the seam open, as in Diagram 3.

5. Pin the other two short sides, right sides together, forming a tube. Extend one corner beyond the edge, the width desired for the bias strip – 3″. See Diagram 4. Stitch in a ¼″ seam.

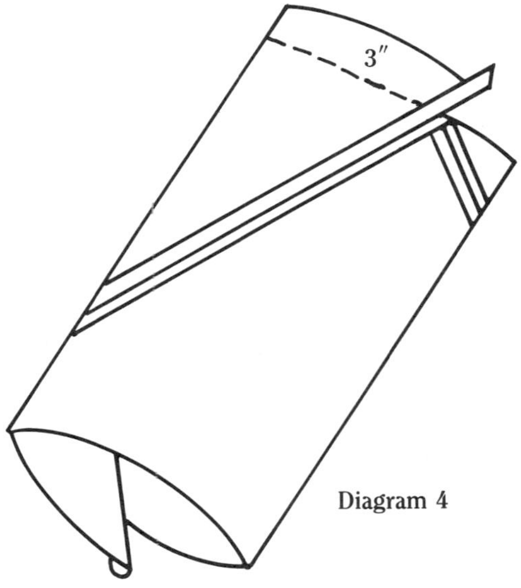

Diagram 4

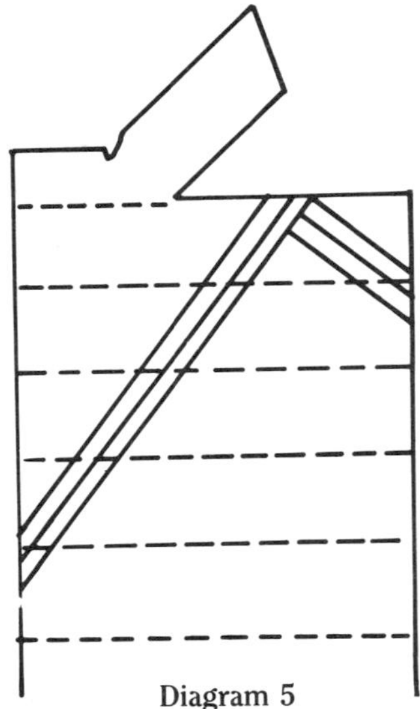
Diagram 5

6. Start at one corner and mark and cut a 3″ wide strip continuously around the fabric tube. See Diagram 5. The most convenient place to do this is on the end of an ironing board.

C. How to apply the binding

1. Trim the quilt backing to match the quilt top.

2. Leave the batting ½″ larger all around in order to fill out the binding.

3. Fold the 3″ bias in half lengthwise, wrong sides together. Begin on the center of a side (to avoid bulky seams near the corner) and pin the bias to the quilt top with the raw edges flush. Sew a ¼″ seam through all five layers.

4. Stitch up to the seam line at each corner. Lift the needle, leave a small amount of fabric (about 5″ to 6″), and reinsert the needle for stitching the next side.

5. Turn the folded edge of the bias to the quilt back and whipstitch to the back. Trim and miter the corners.

Bibliography
Recommended References

A. For Basic Quiltmaking Instructions

Beyer, Jinny. *Patchwork Patterns.* McLean, Va.: EPM Publications, Inc., 1979.

Hassel, Carla J. *Super Quilter II.* Lombard, Ill.: Wallace-Homestead Book Company, 1982.

__________, *You Can Be a Super Quilter.* Lombard, Ill.: Wallace-Homestead Book Company, 1980.

Ickis, Marguerite. *The Standard Book of Quilt Making And Collecting.* 1949. Reprint. New York: Dover Publications, 1959.

James, Michael. *The Quiltmaker's Handbook.* Englewood Cliffs, N.J.: Prentice-Hall, Inc., 1978.

Lady's Circle Patchwork Quilts. New York: Lopez Publications.

Leone, Diana. *The Sampler Quilt.* Los Altos, Calif.: Leone Publishing Co., 1980.

MacDonald, Jessie. *Let's Make More Patchwork Quilts.* Philadelphia: Farm Journal, Inc., 1984.

__________, and Marian H. Shafer. *Let's Make a Patchwork Quilt.* Philadelphia: Farm Journal, Inc., 1980.

B. For Additional Pattern Ideas

Beyer, Jinny. *The Quilter's Album of Blocks & Borders.* McLean, Va.: EPM Publications, Inc., 1980.

Hopkins, Mary Ellen. *The It's Okay If You Sit On My Quilt Book.* Atlanta: Yours Truly, Inc., 1982.

McKim, Ruby. *101 Patchwork Patterns.* 1931. Reprint. New York: Dover Publications, Inc., 1962.

Mills, Susan Winter. *Illustrated Index to Traditional American Quilt Patterns.* New York: Arco Publishing, Inc., 1981.

Quilter's Newsletter Magazine. Wheatridge, Colo.: Leman Publications.

C. For History, Nostalgia, and Inspiration

Binney, Edward, 3rd, and Gail Binney-Winslow. *Homage to Amanda.* San Francisco: R.K. Press, 1984.

Holstein, Jonathan. *The Pieced Quilt: An American Design Tradition.* Boston: New York Graphic Society, 1973.

Kentucky Quilts 1800-1900. New York: Pantheon Books, 1982.

The Quilt Digest. Volumes 1, 2, 3 and 4. San Francisco: The Quilt Digest Press, 1983-1986.

Pellman, Rachel and Kenneth. *The World of Amish Quilts.* Intercourse, Penn.: Good Books, 1984.

About the Author

Judy Florence is a quilt designer, teacher, writer, and award-winning quiltmaker. Her quilts, designs, and articles have been featured in many quilt magazines, needlework periodicals, and calendars. She has won numerous awards in Midwestern and national shows, including first place in the Wisconsin Historical Society Quilt Contest and Best Quilt with American Indian Influence at the International Quilt Exhibit in California.

Judy makes her home in Eau Claire, Wisconsin, with her husband Dick and their sons Matthew and David. They enjoy reading, music and travel.

Templates

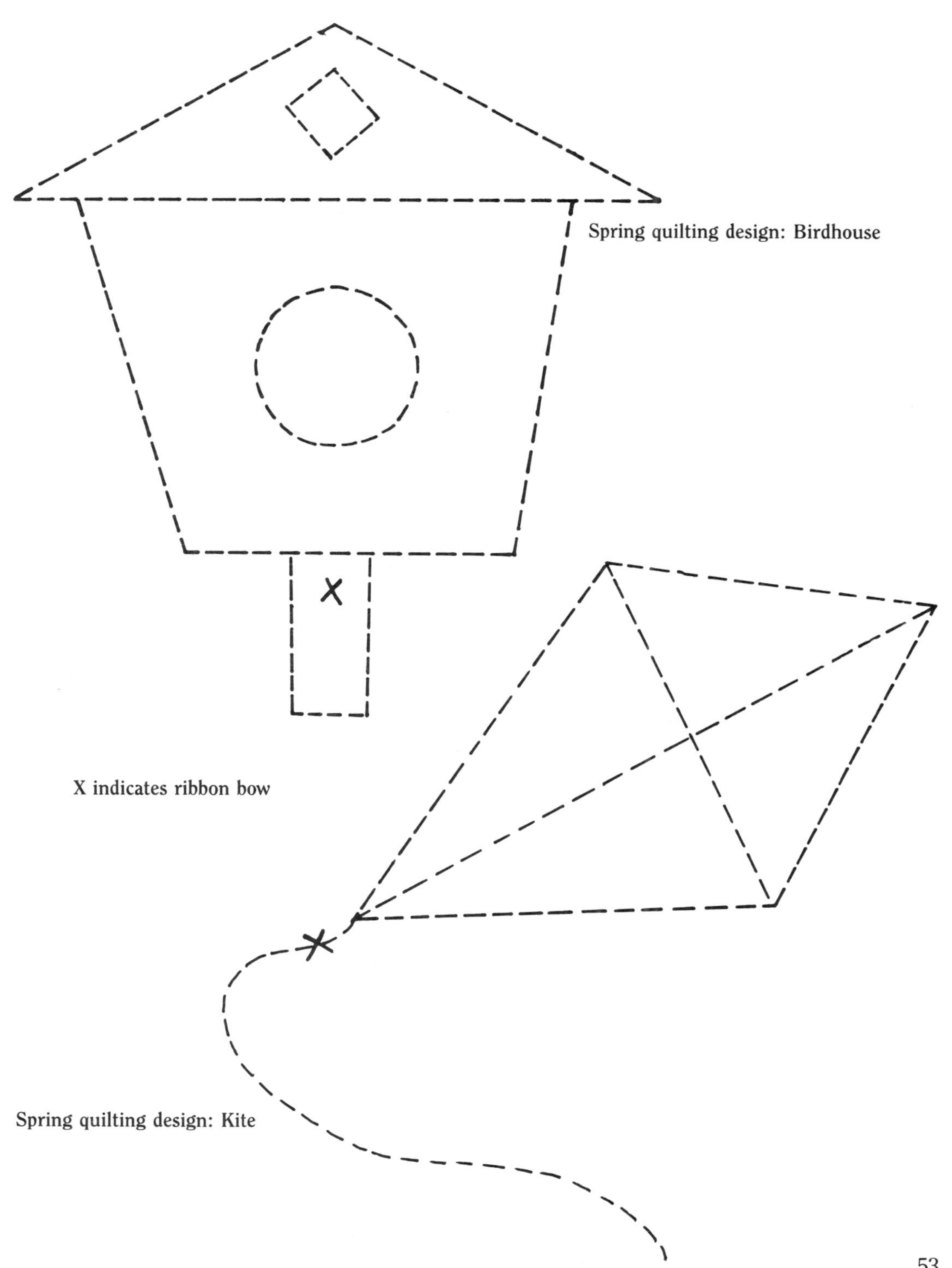

Spring quilting design: Birdhouse

X indicates ribbon bow

Spring quilting design: Kite

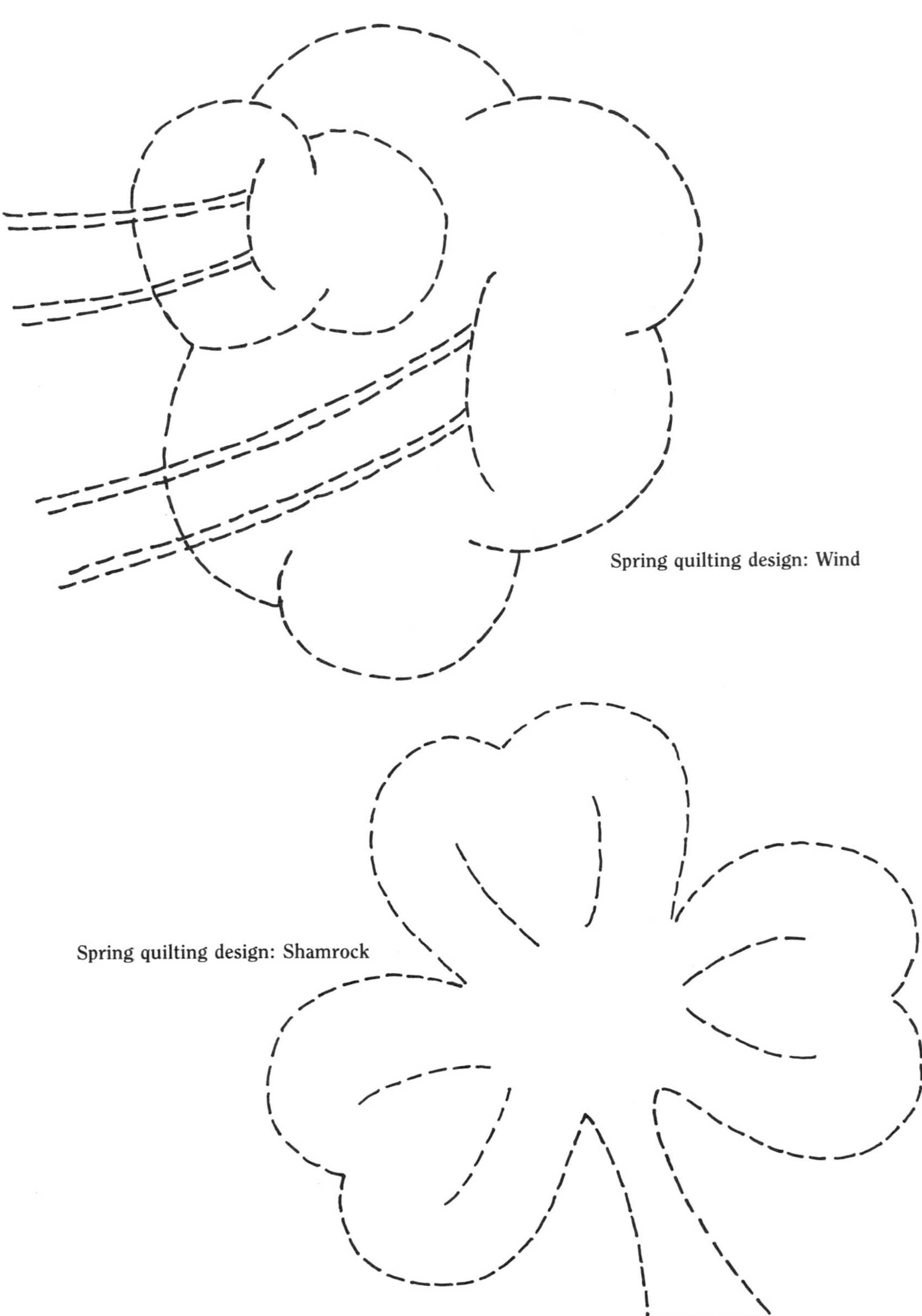

Spring quilting design: Wind

Spring quilting design: Shamrock

X indicates location for ribbon bow.

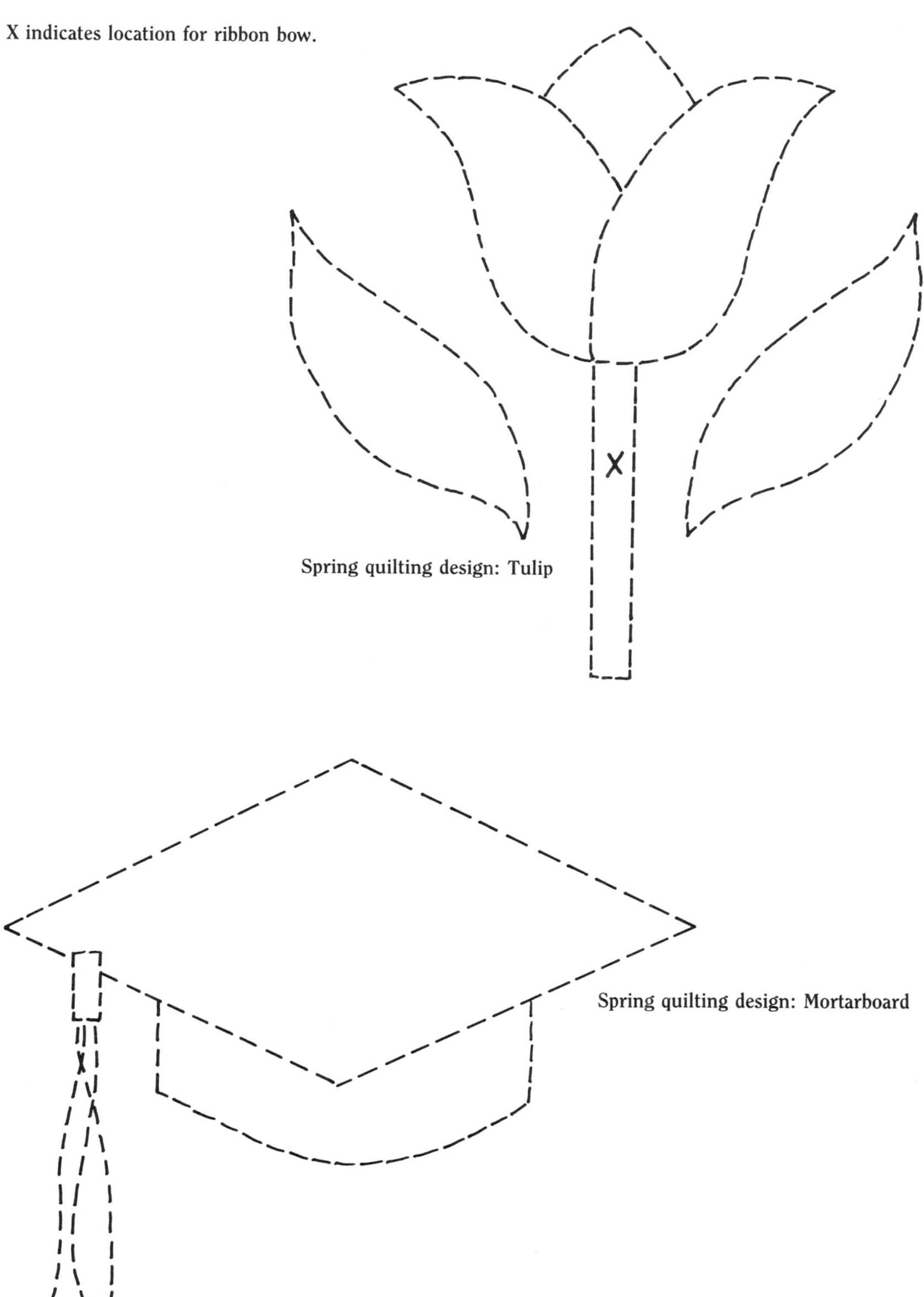

Spring quilting design: Tulip

Spring quilting design: Mortarboard

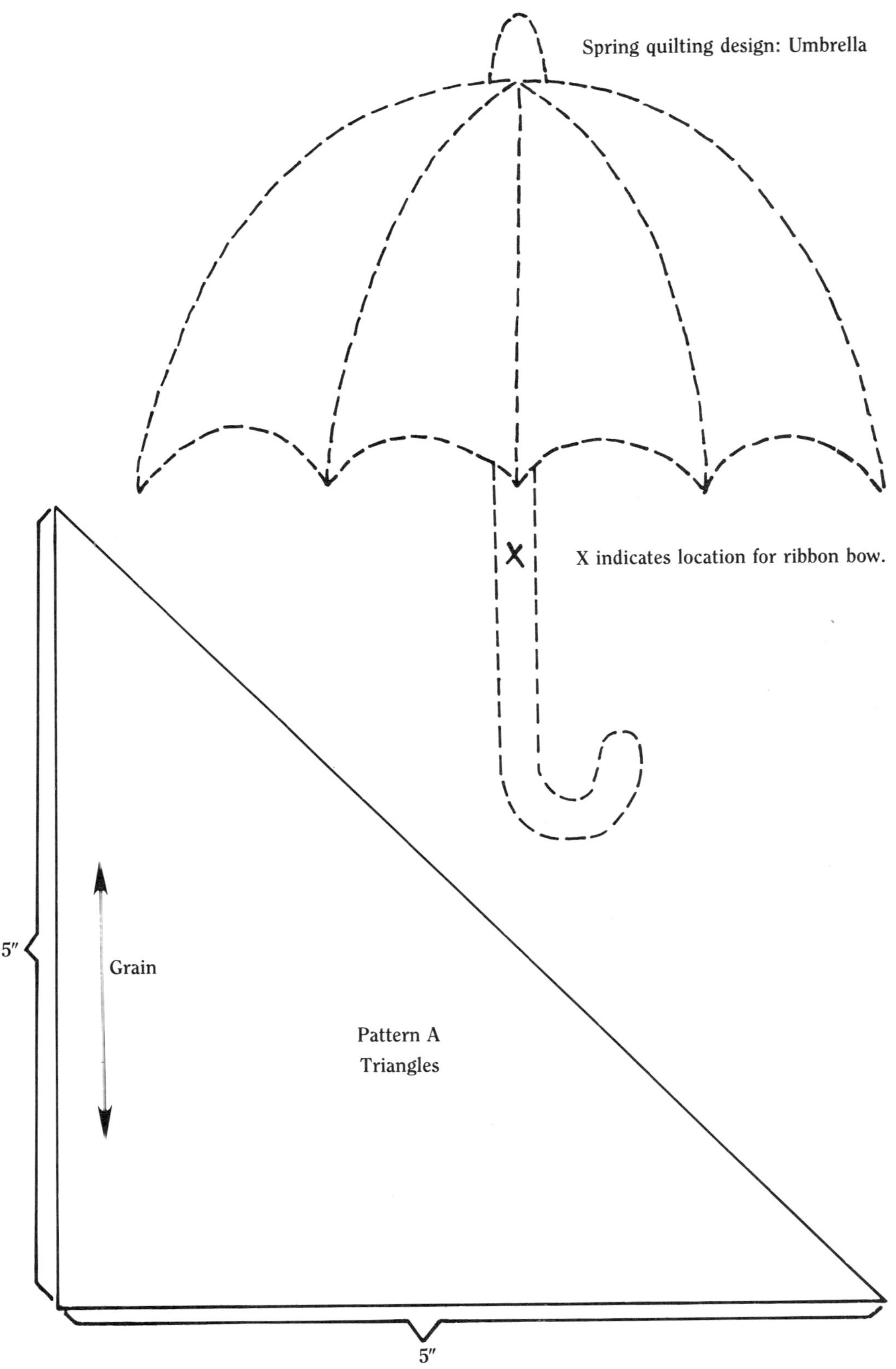
Spring quilting design: Umbrella
X
X indicates location for ribbon bow.
5″
Grain
Pattern A
Triangles
5″

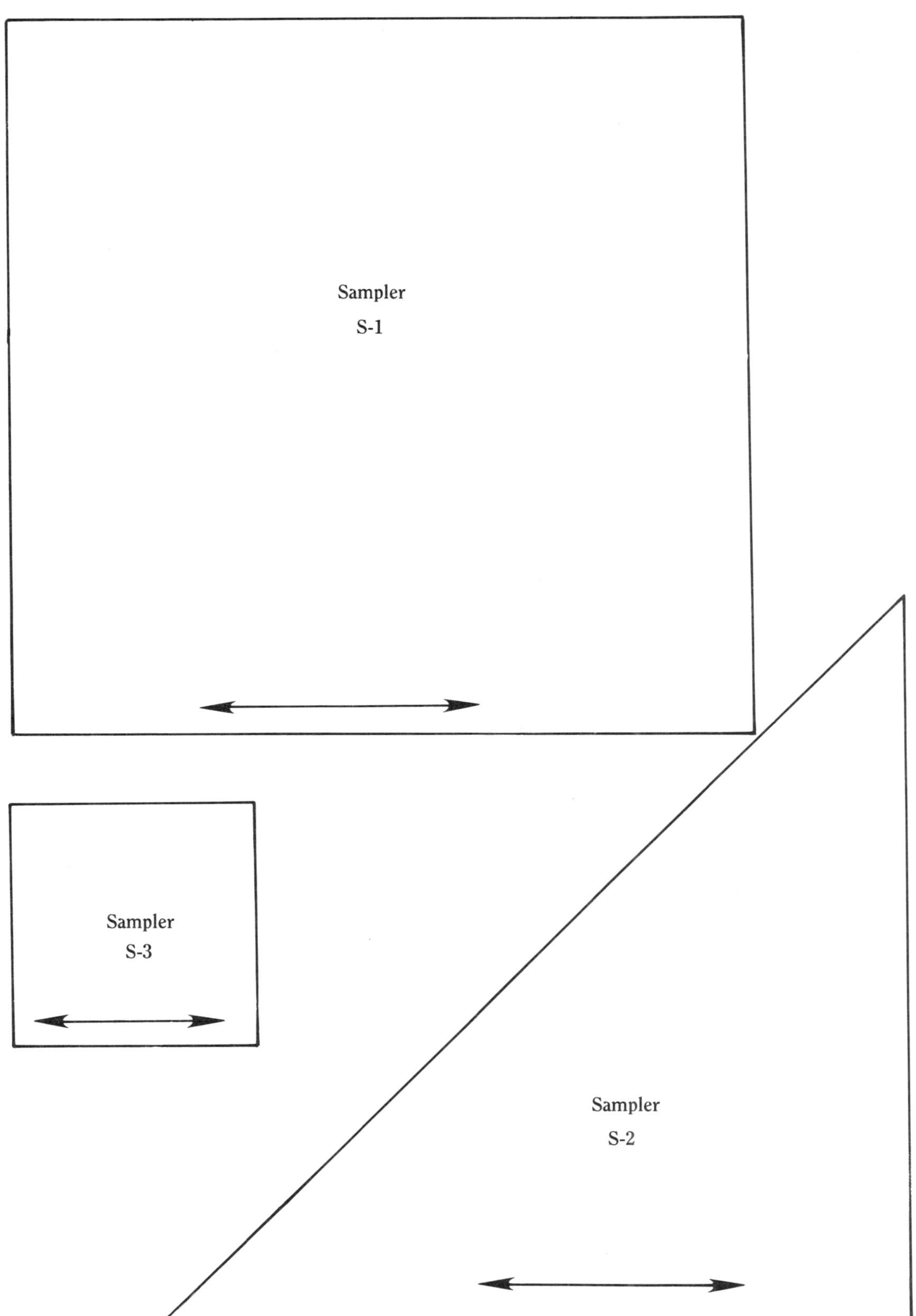
Sampler
S-1
Sampler
S-3
Sampler
S-2

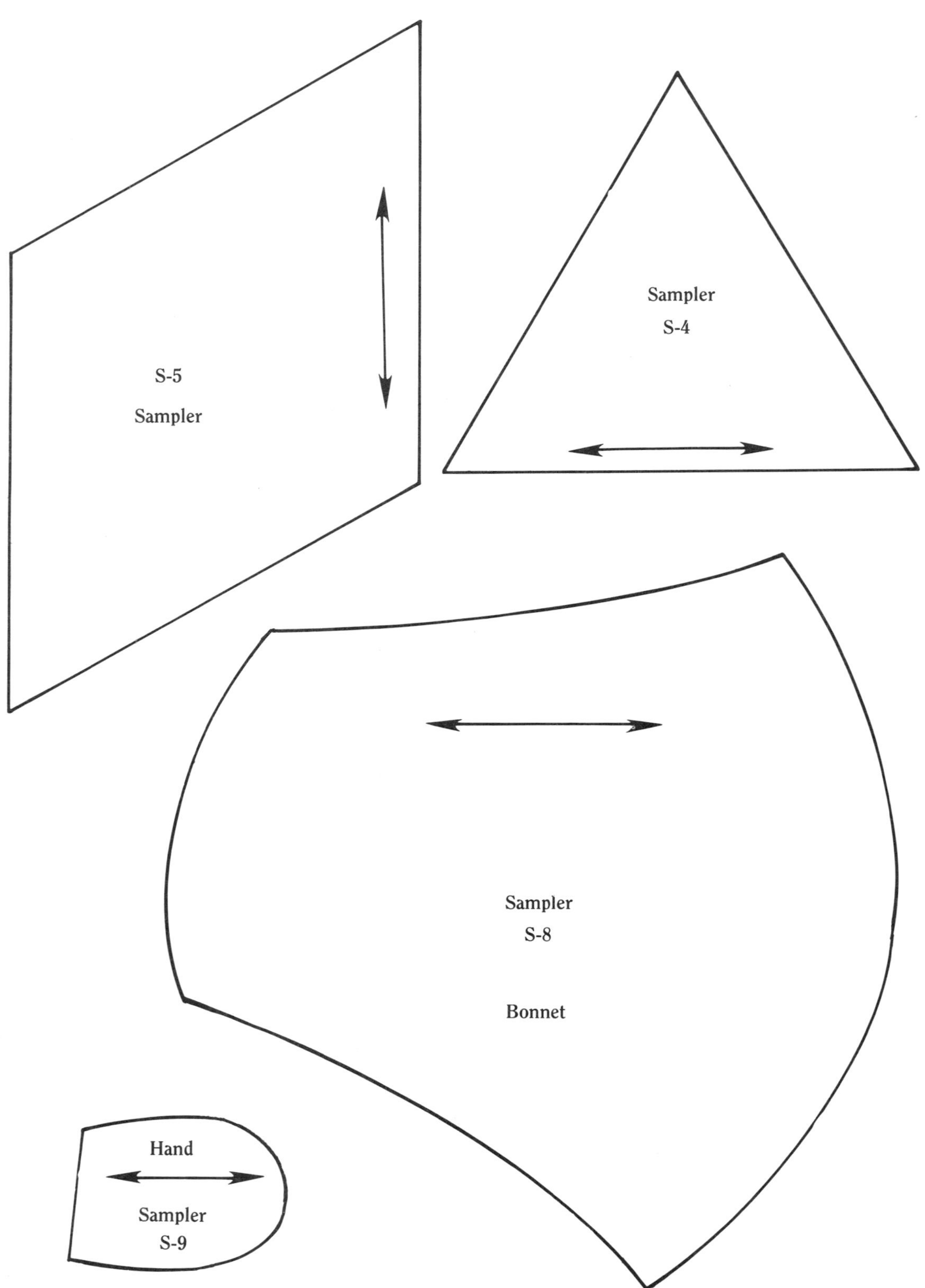
S-5
Sampler
Sampler
S-4
Sampler
S-8
Bonnet
Hand
Sampler
S-9

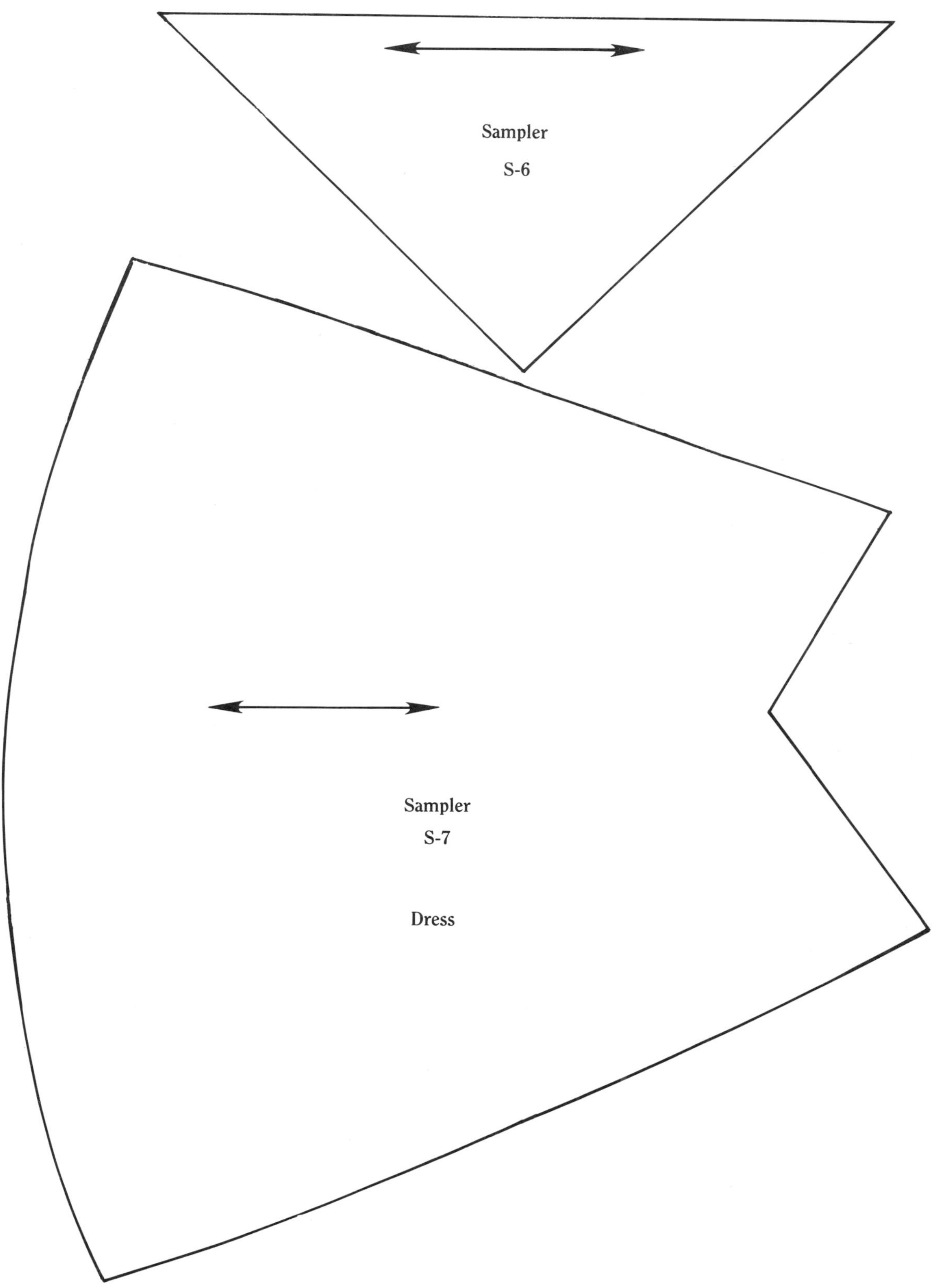
Sampler
S-6
Sampler
S-7
Dress

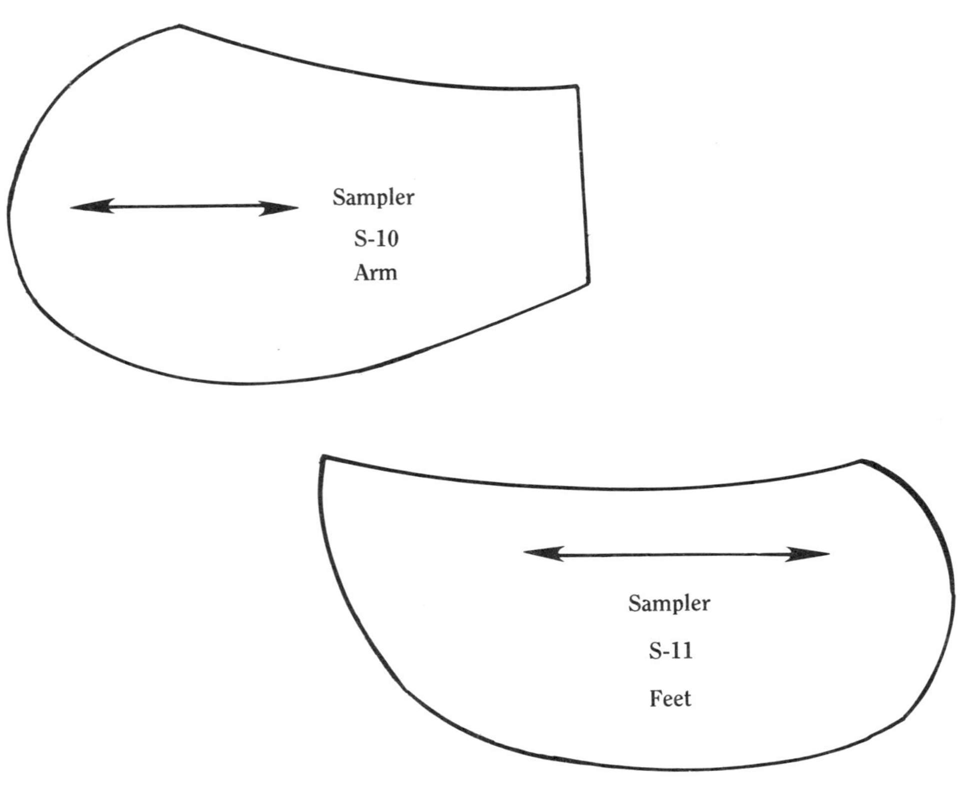
Sampler
S-10
Arm
Sampler
S-11
Feet

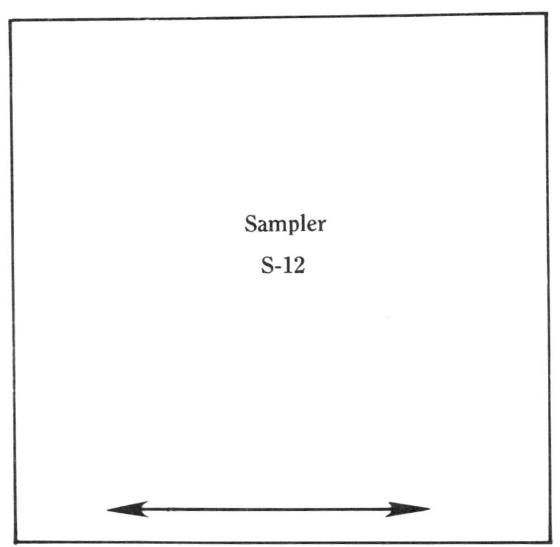
Sampler
S-12

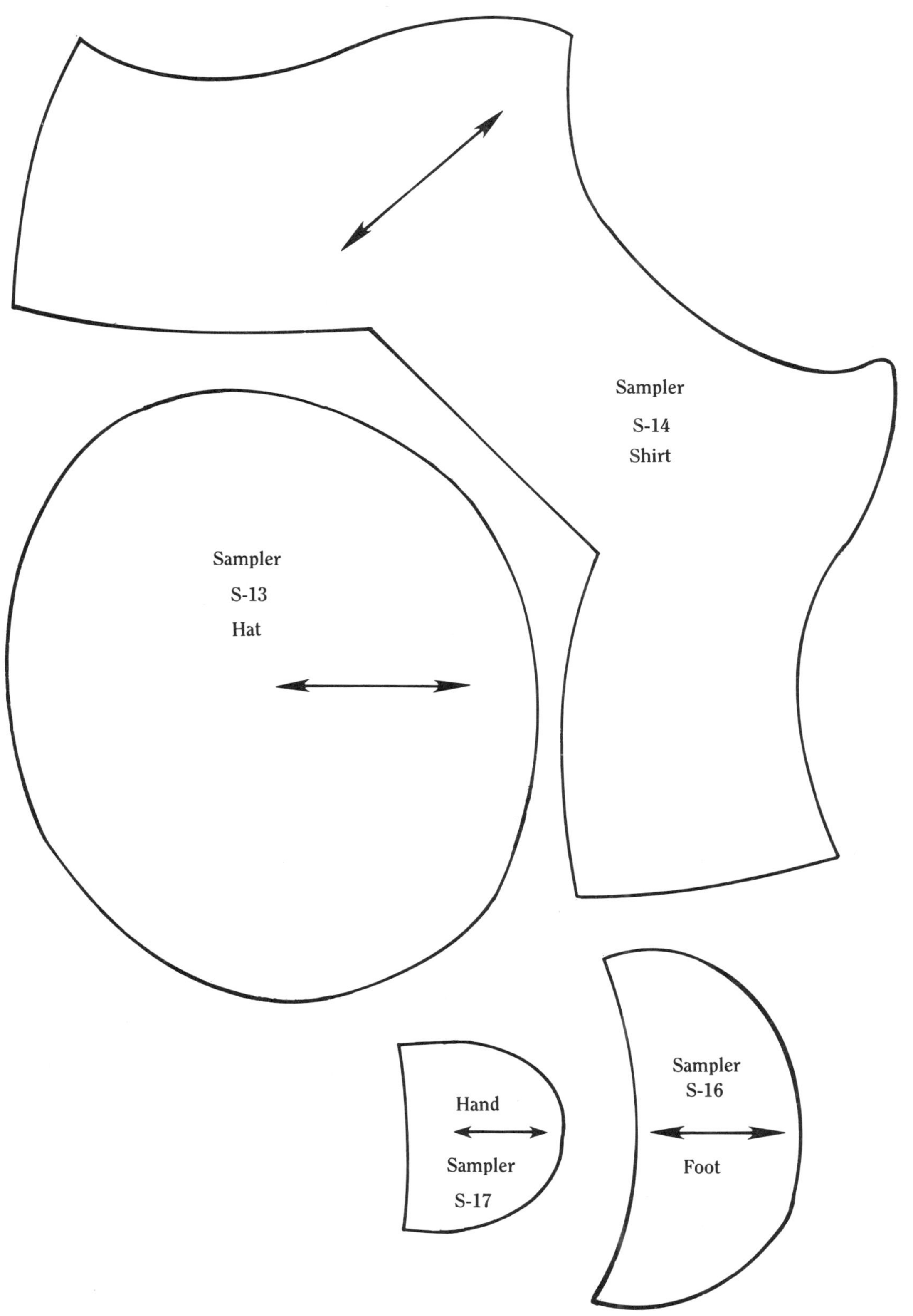
Sampler
S-14
Shirt
Sampler
S-13
Hat
Sampler
S-16
Hand
Sampler
S-17
Foot

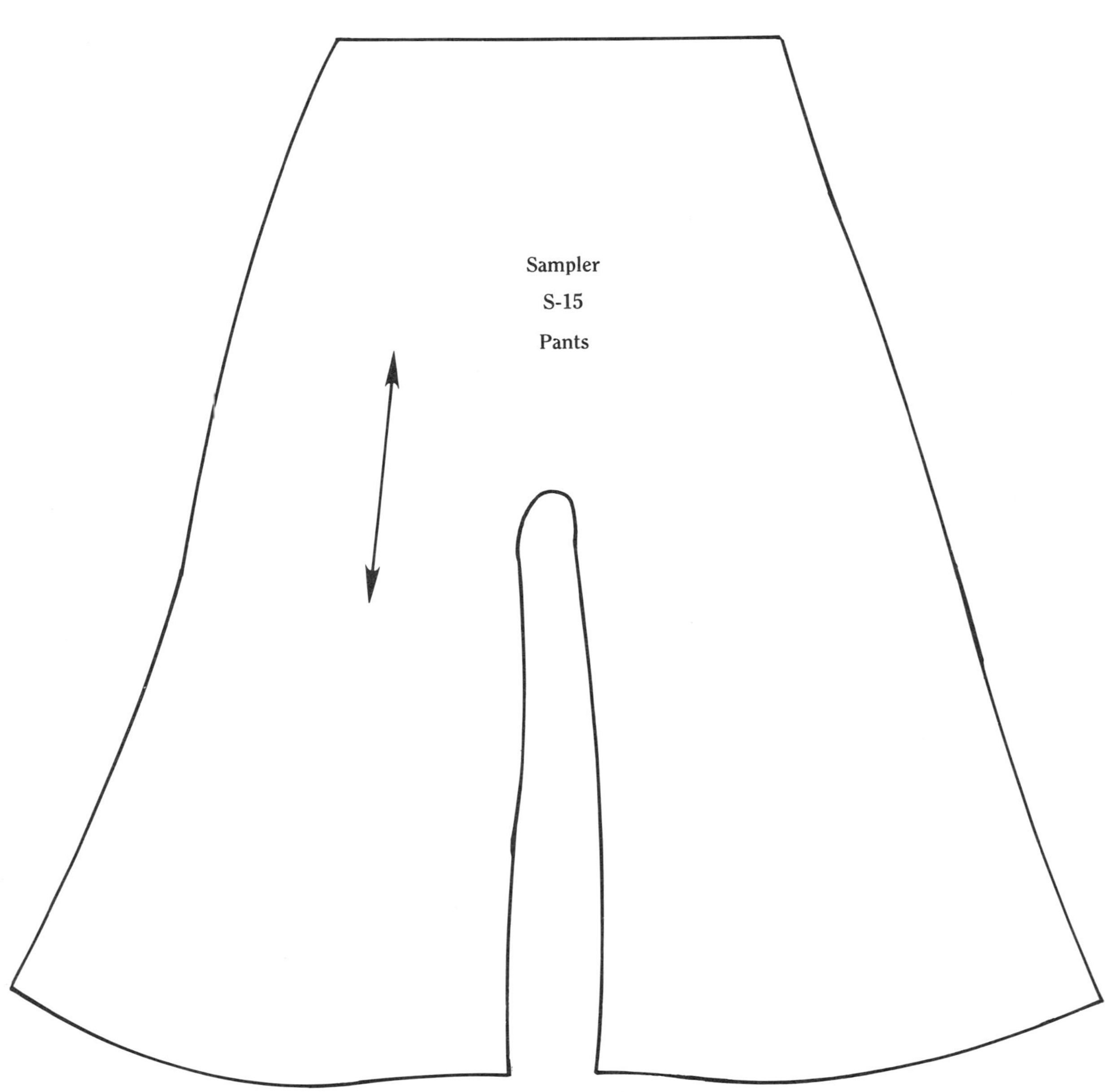
Sampler
S-15
Pants

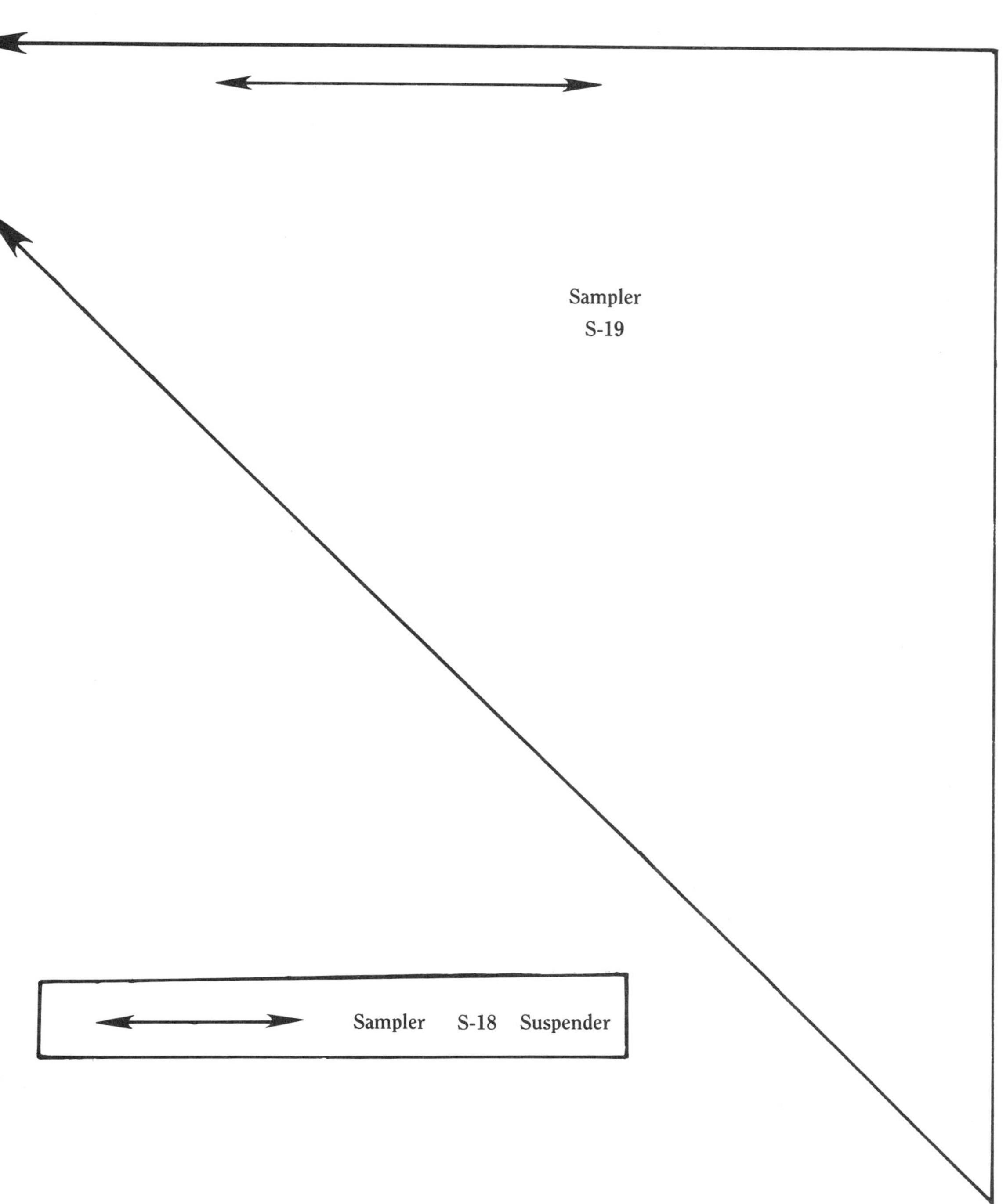
Sampler
S-19
Sampler S-18 Suspender

Sampler
S-20

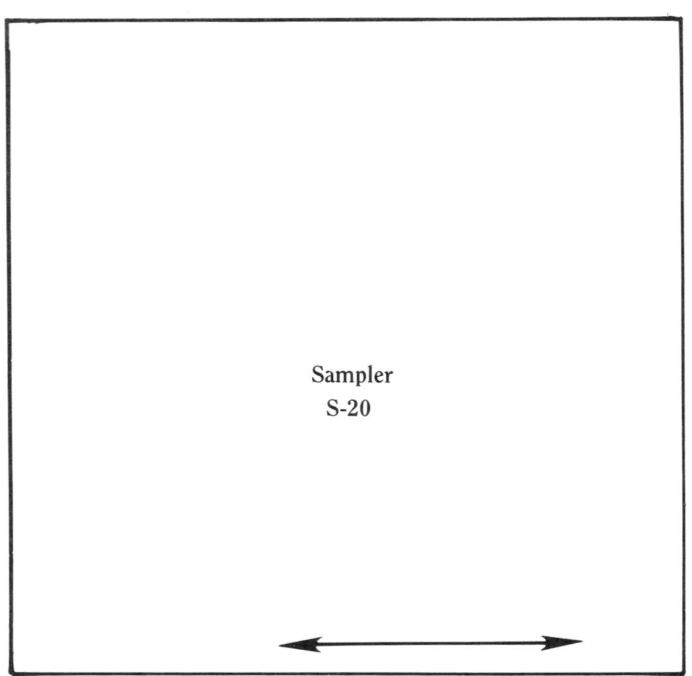

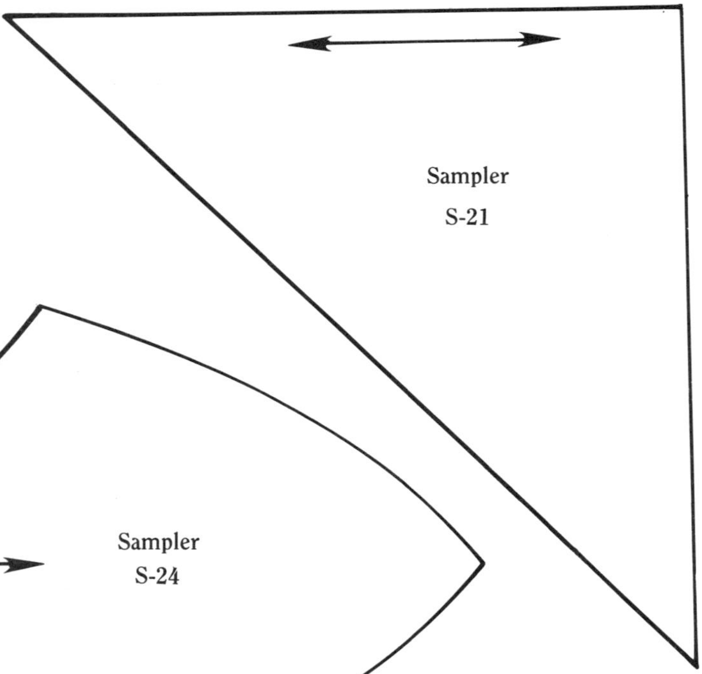

Sampler
S-21

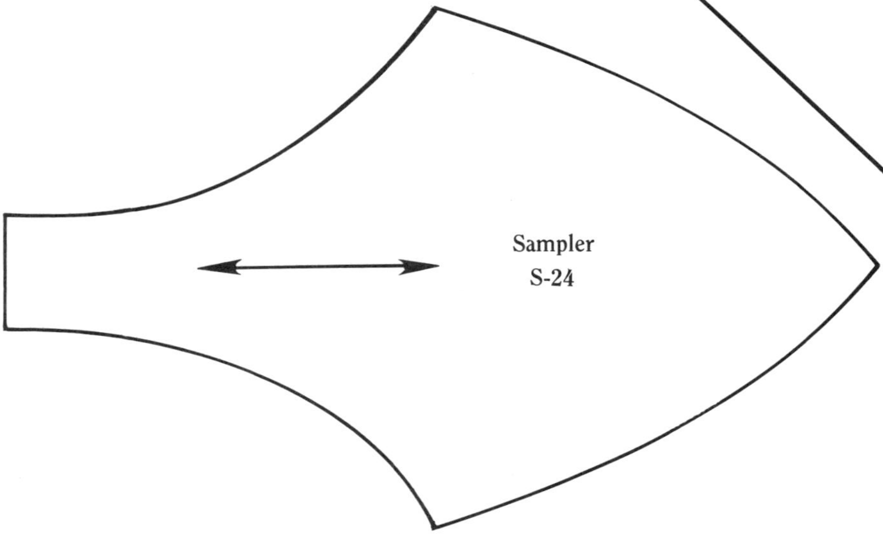

Sampler
S-24

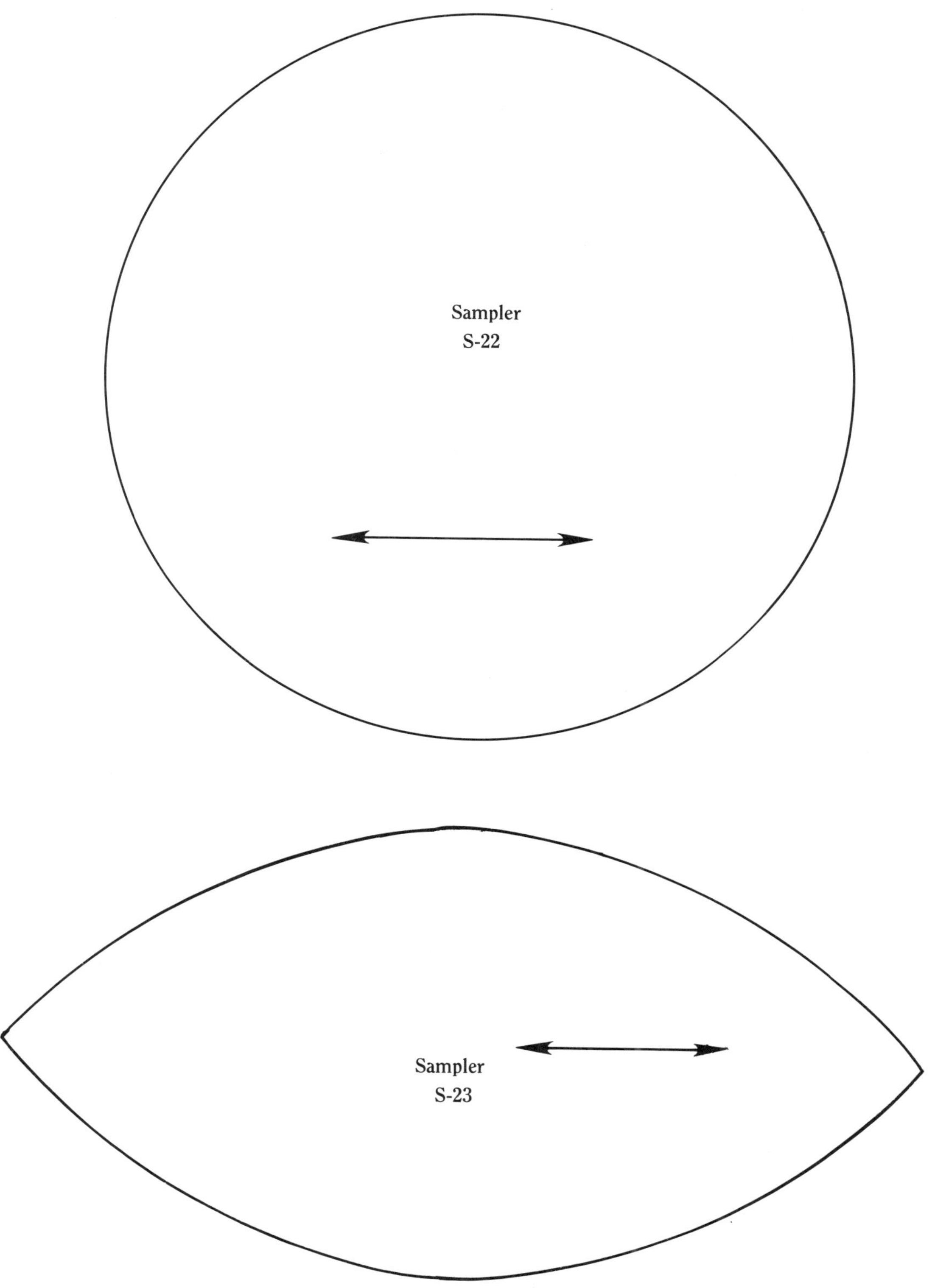
Sampler
S-22
Sampler
S-23

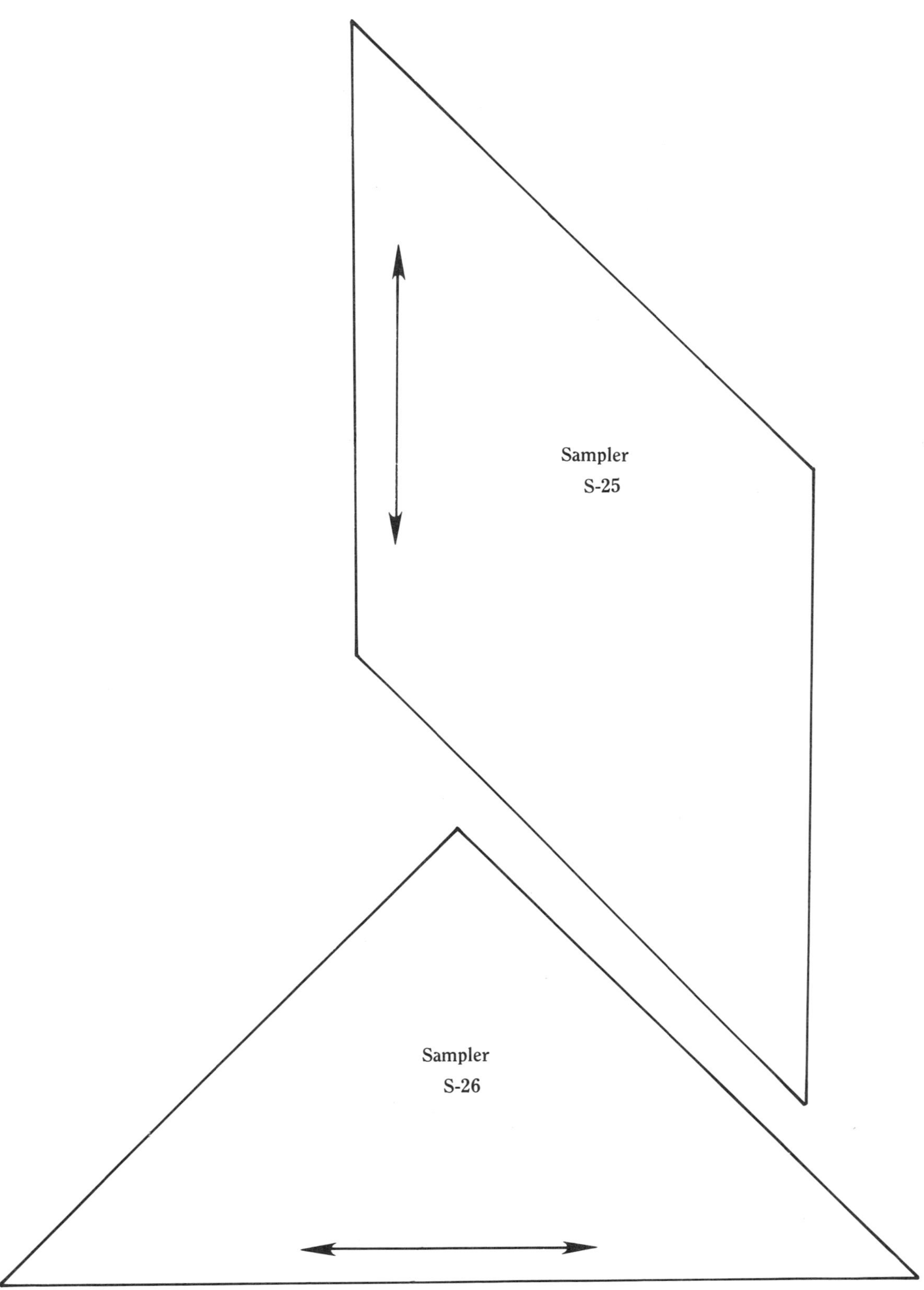
Sampler
S-25
Sampler
S-26

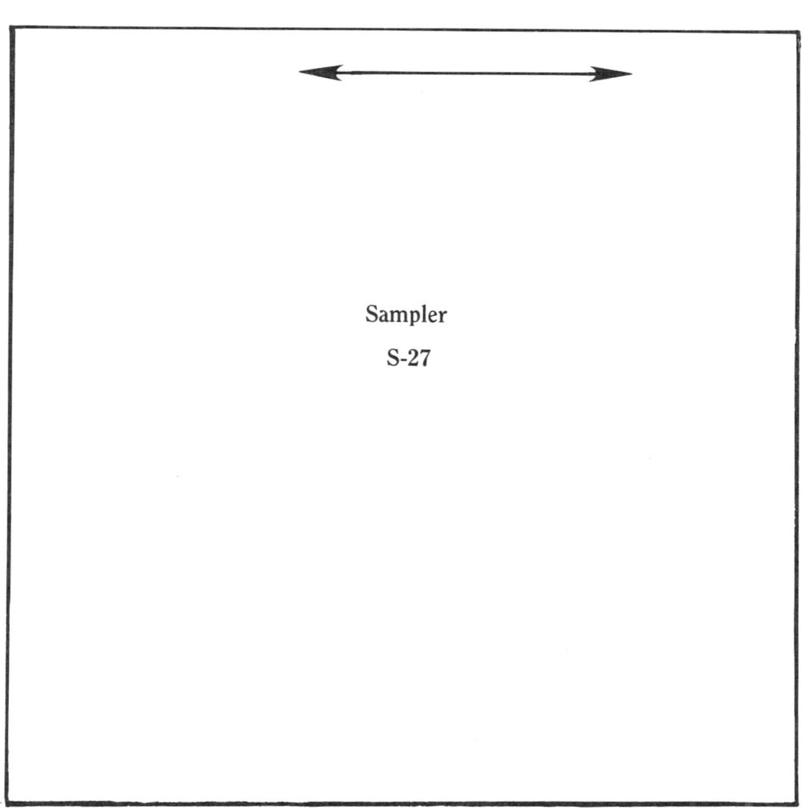
Sampler
S-27

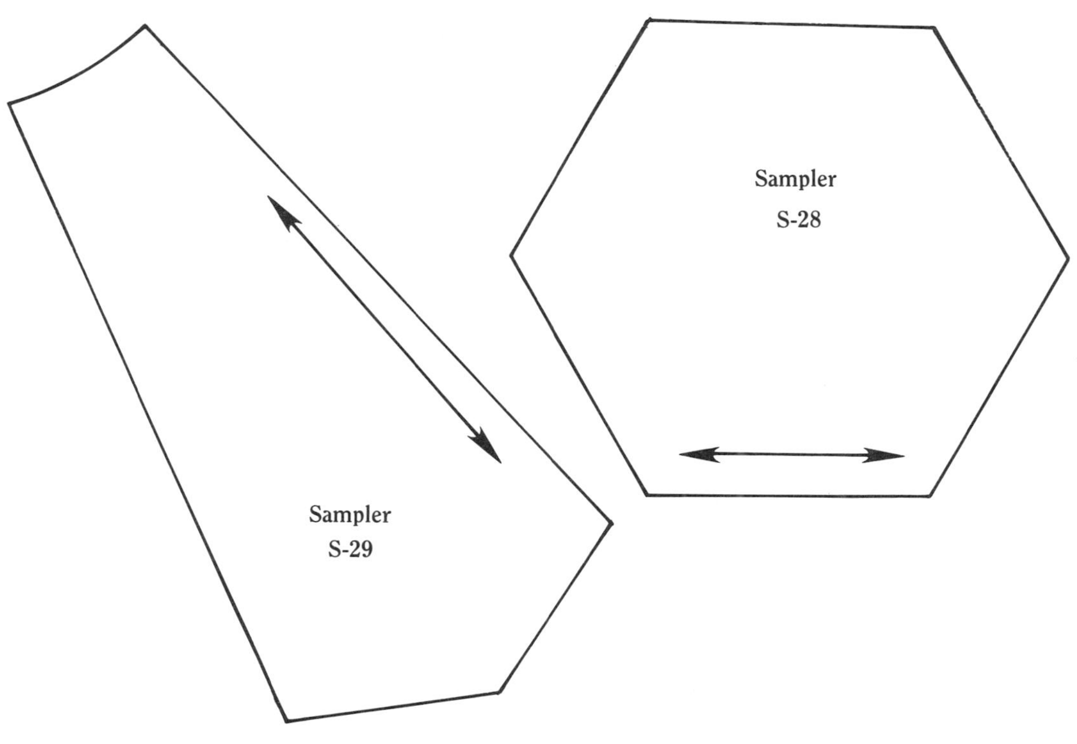
Sampler
S-28
Sampler
S-29

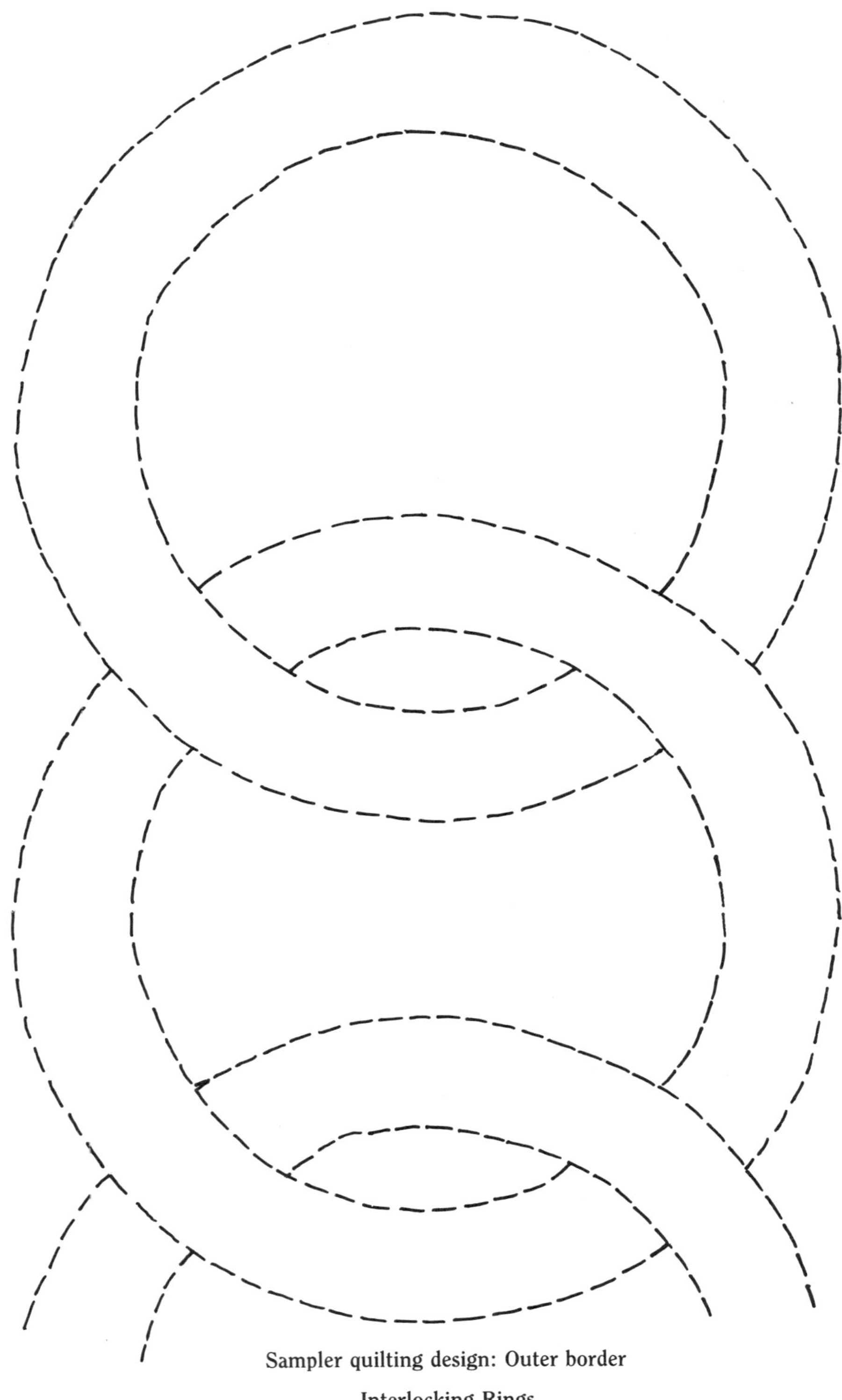

Sampler quilting design: Outer border

Interlocking Rings

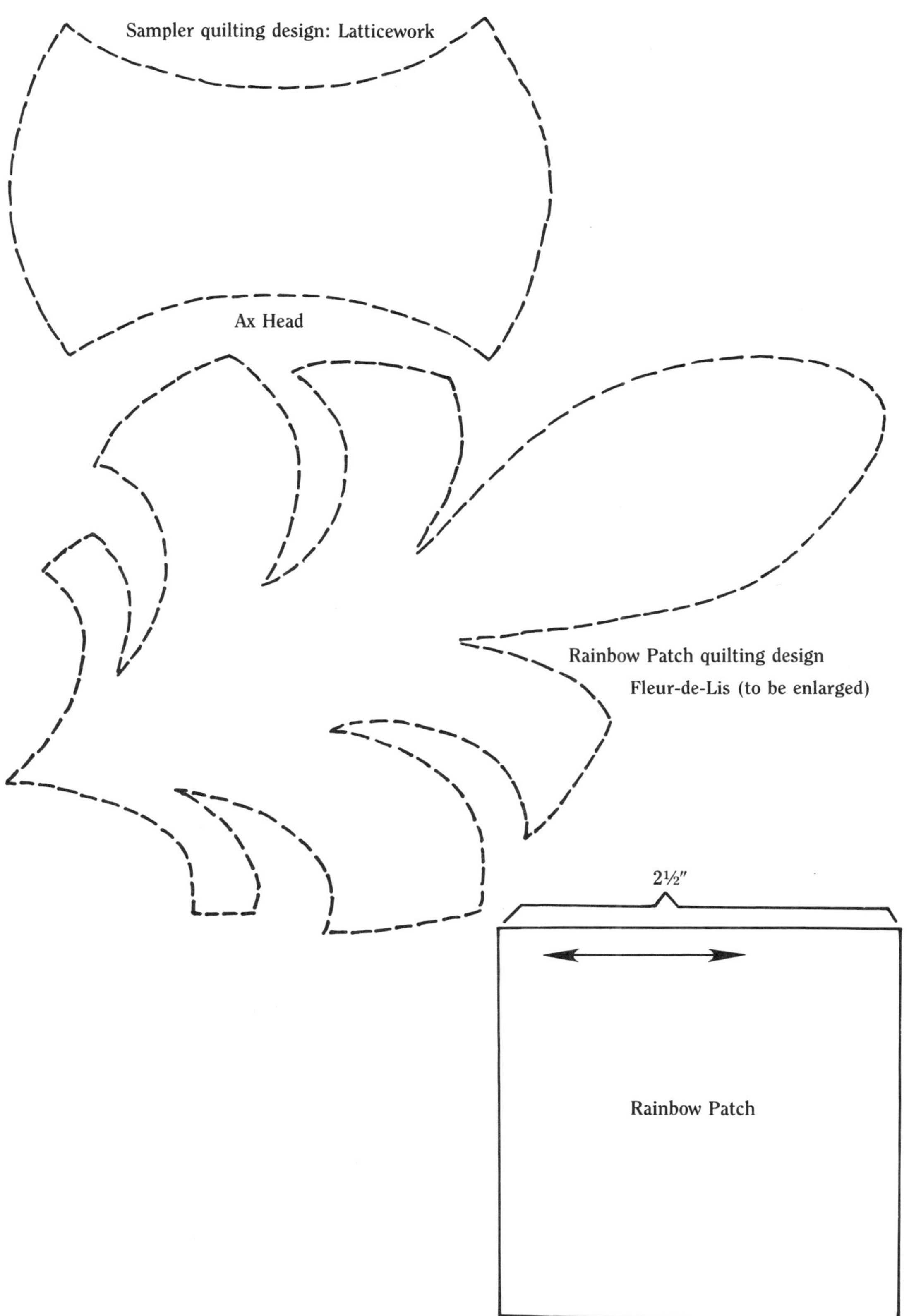
Sampler quilting design: Latticework
Ax Head
Rainbow Patch quilting design
Fleur-de-Lis (to be enlarged)
2½″
Rainbow Patch

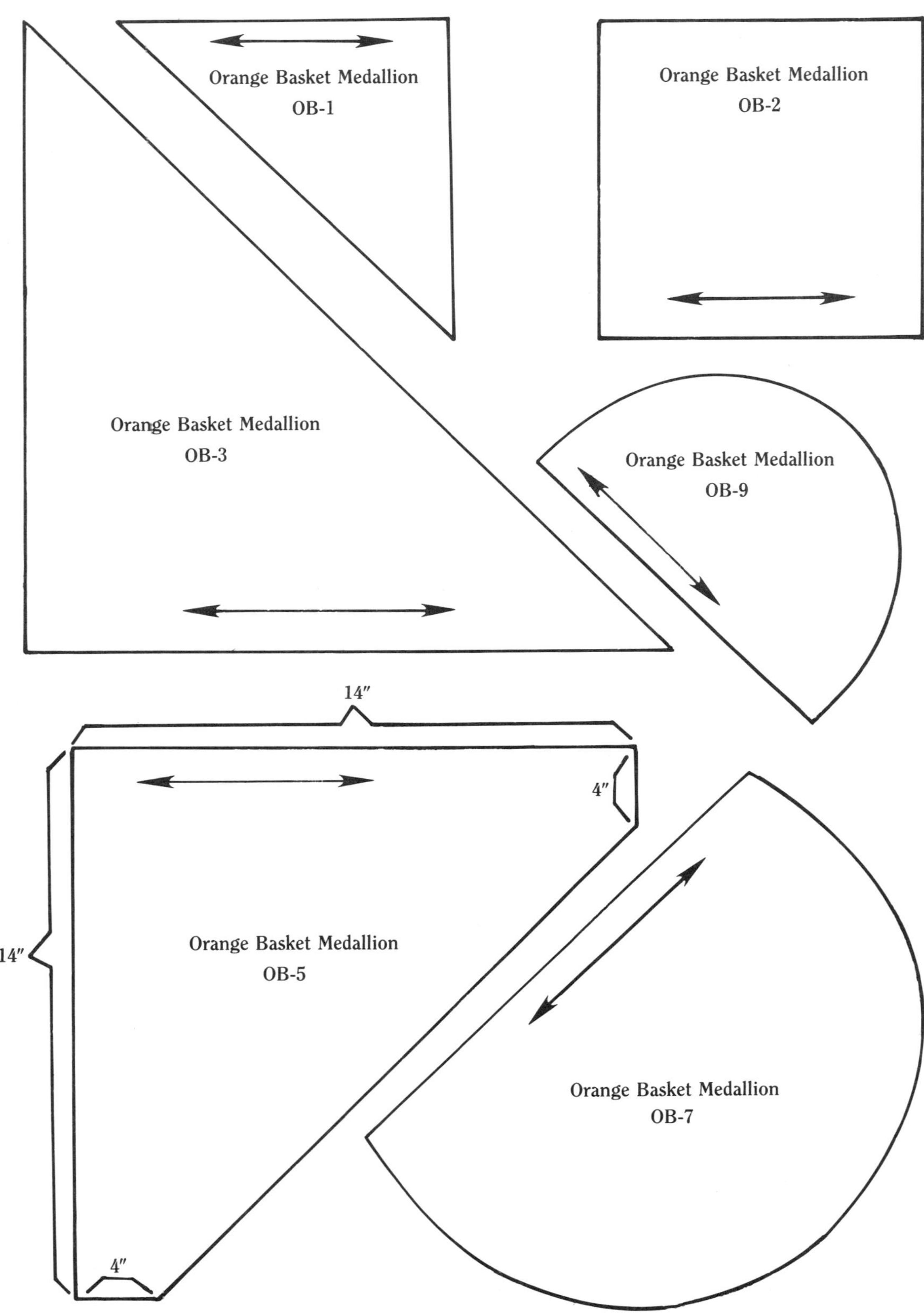
Orange Basket Medallion
OB-1
Orange Basket Medallion
OB-2
Orange Basket Medallion
OB-3
Orange Basket Medallion
OB-9
14″
4″
14″
Orange Basket Medallion
OB-5
4″
Orange Basket Medallion
OB-7

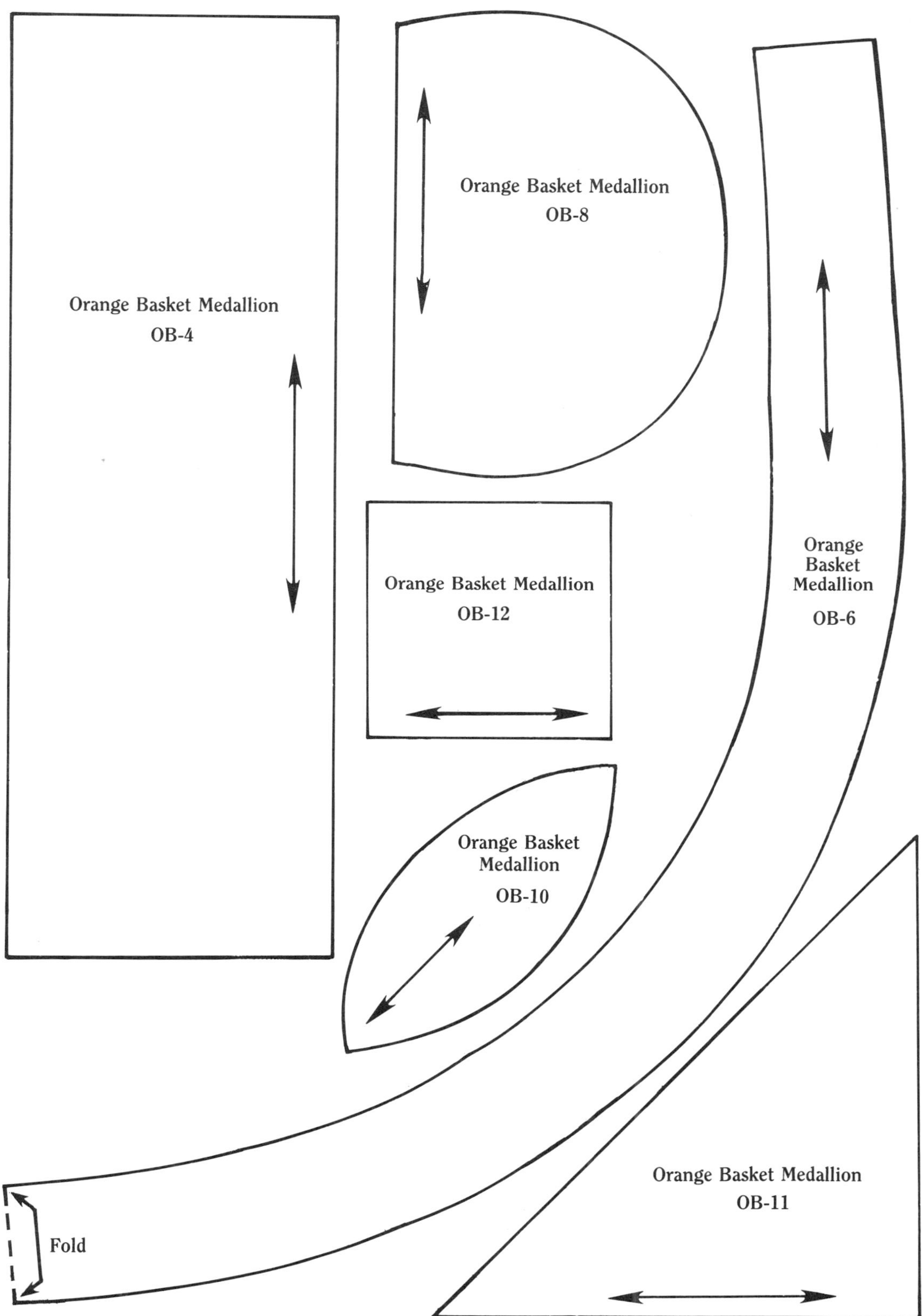
Orange Basket Medallion
OB-4
Orange Basket Medallion
OB-8
Orange Basket Medallion
OB-12
Orange
Basket
Medallion
OB-6
Orange Basket
Medallion
OB-10
Fold
Orange Basket Medallion
OB-11

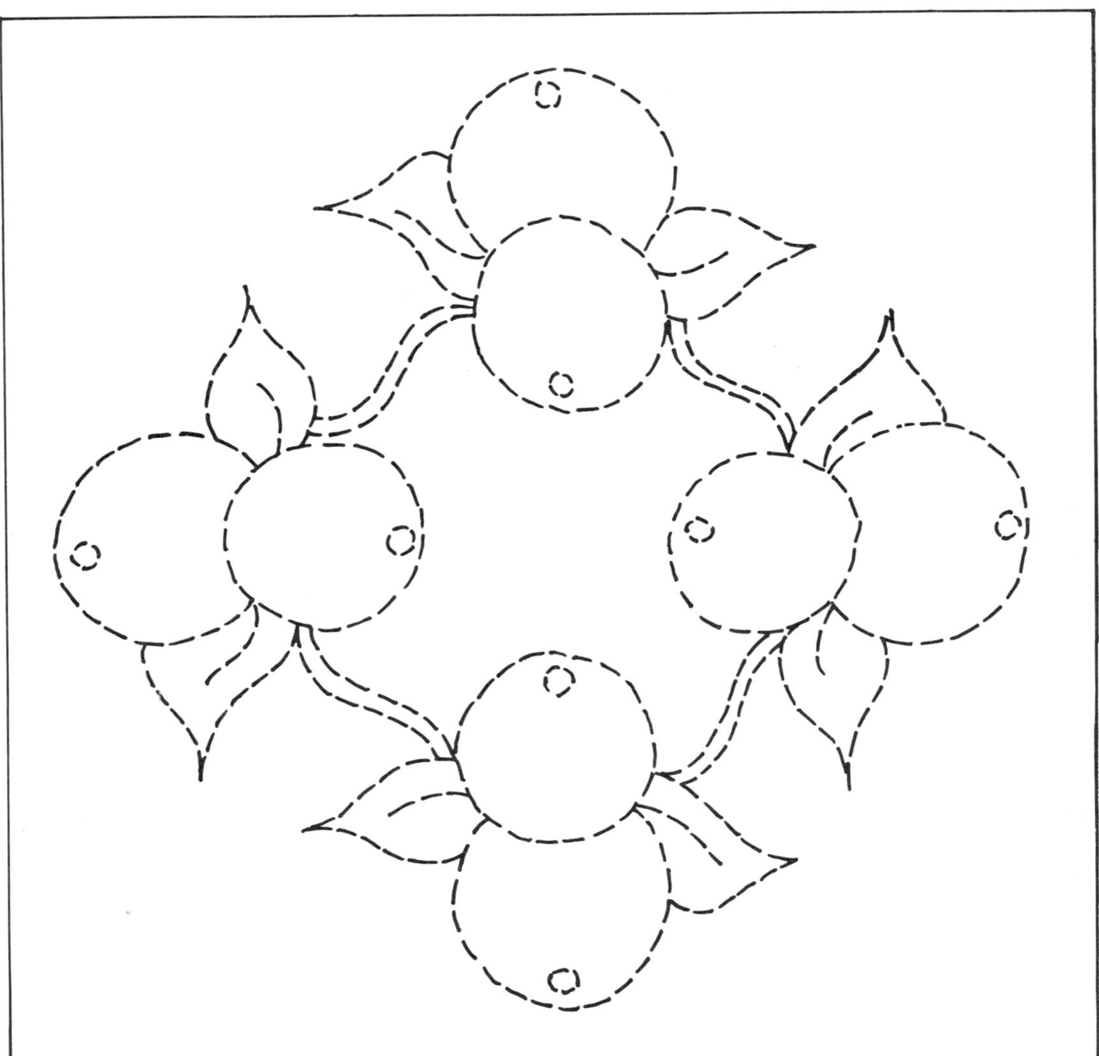

Orange Basket Medallion quilting design (center)

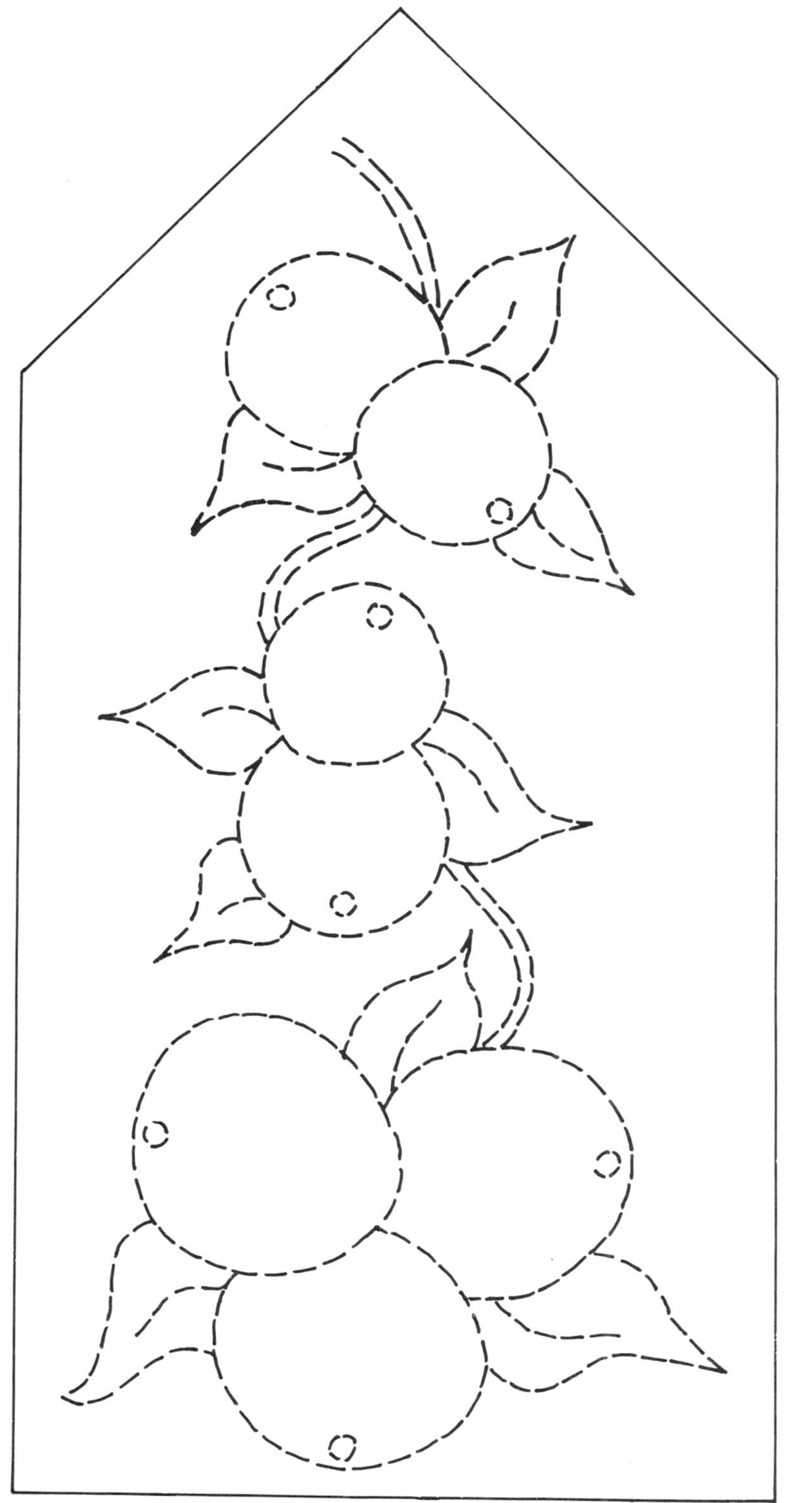

Orange Basket Medallion quilting design (between baskets)

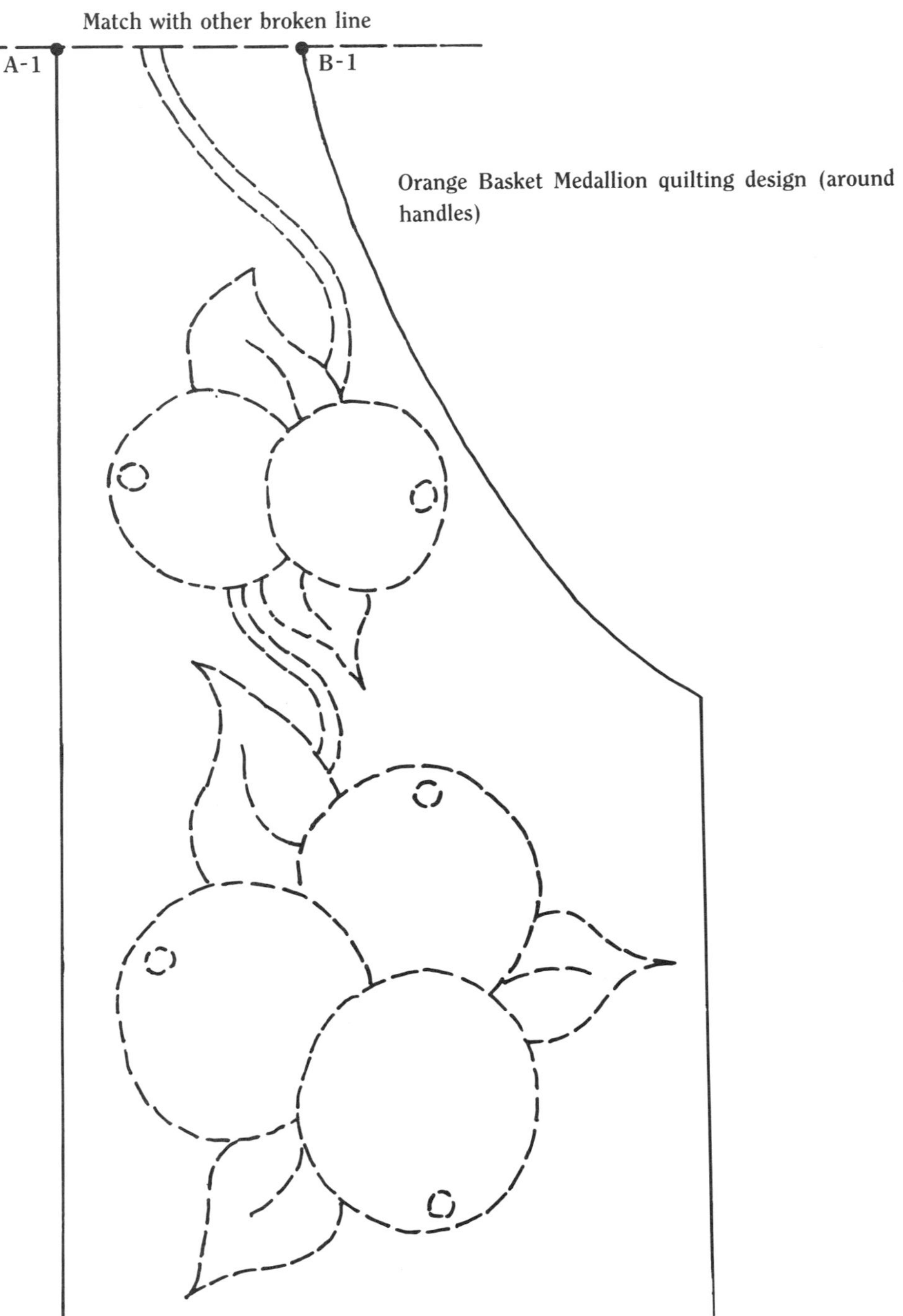

Orange Basket Medallion quilting design (around handles)

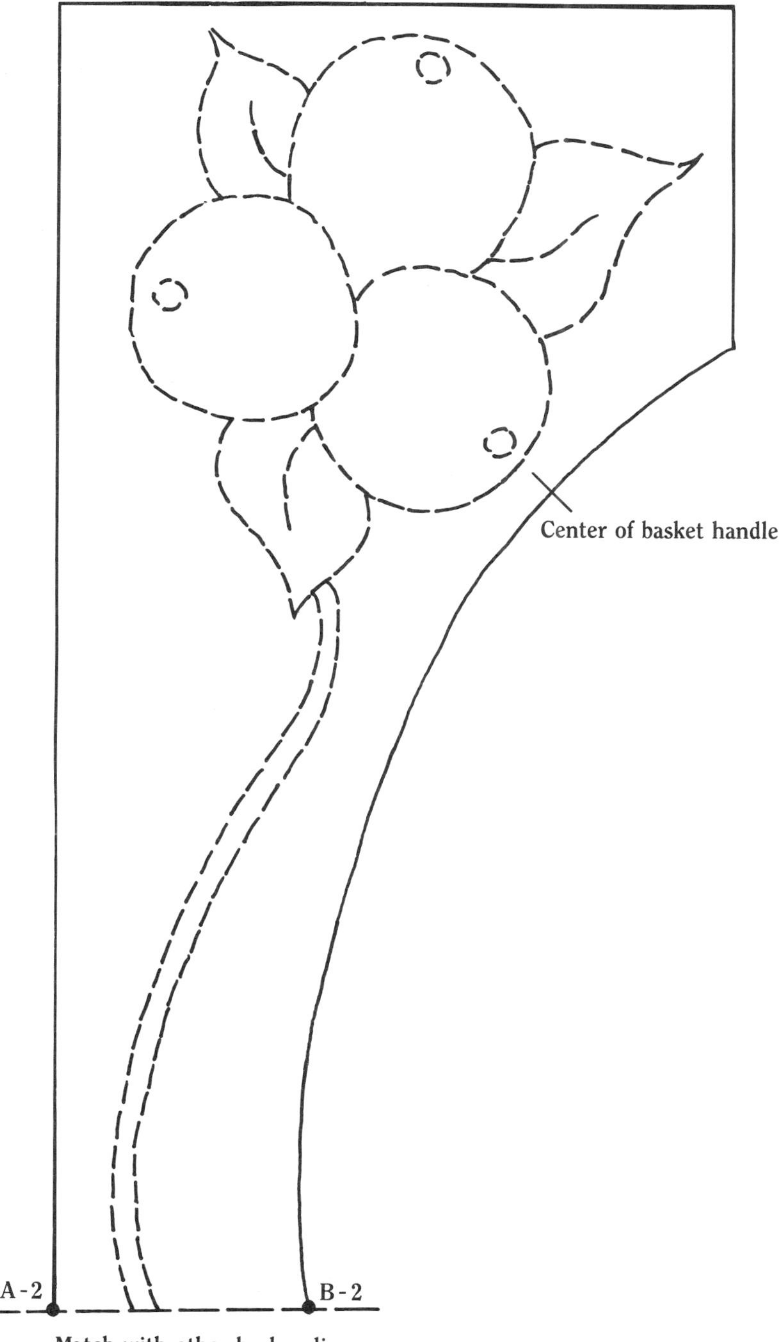
Center of basket handle
A-2
B-2
Match with other broken line

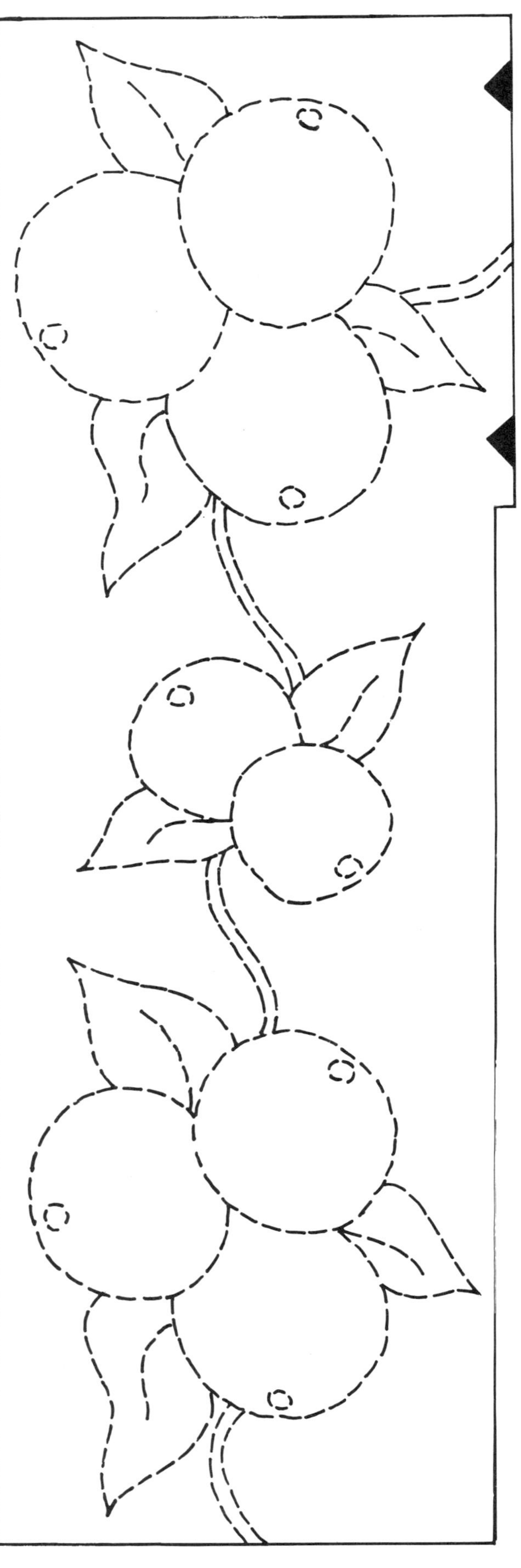

Join at notches

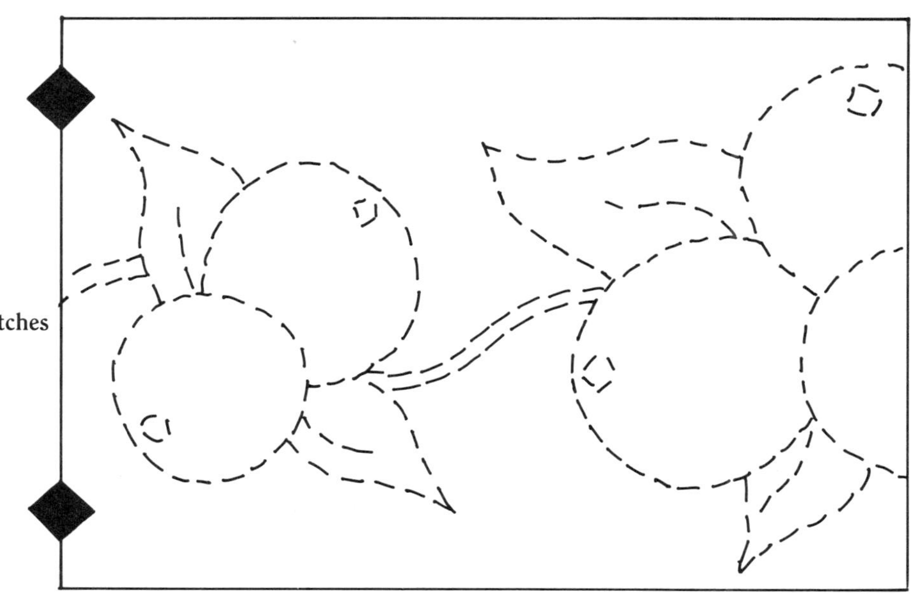

Orange Basket Medallion quilting design (borders)

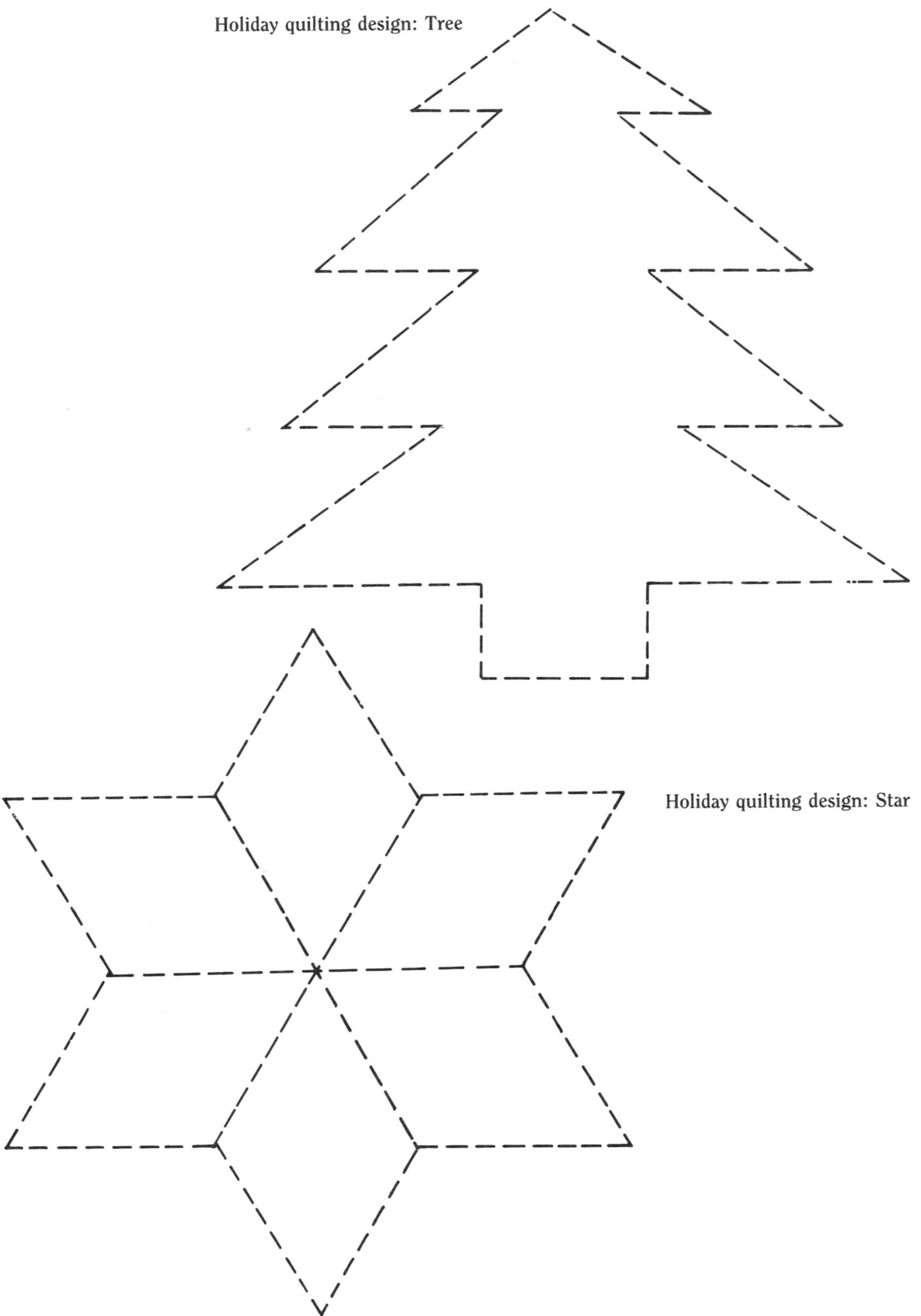

Holiday quilting design: Tree

Holiday quilting design: Star

X indicates location for ribbon bow.

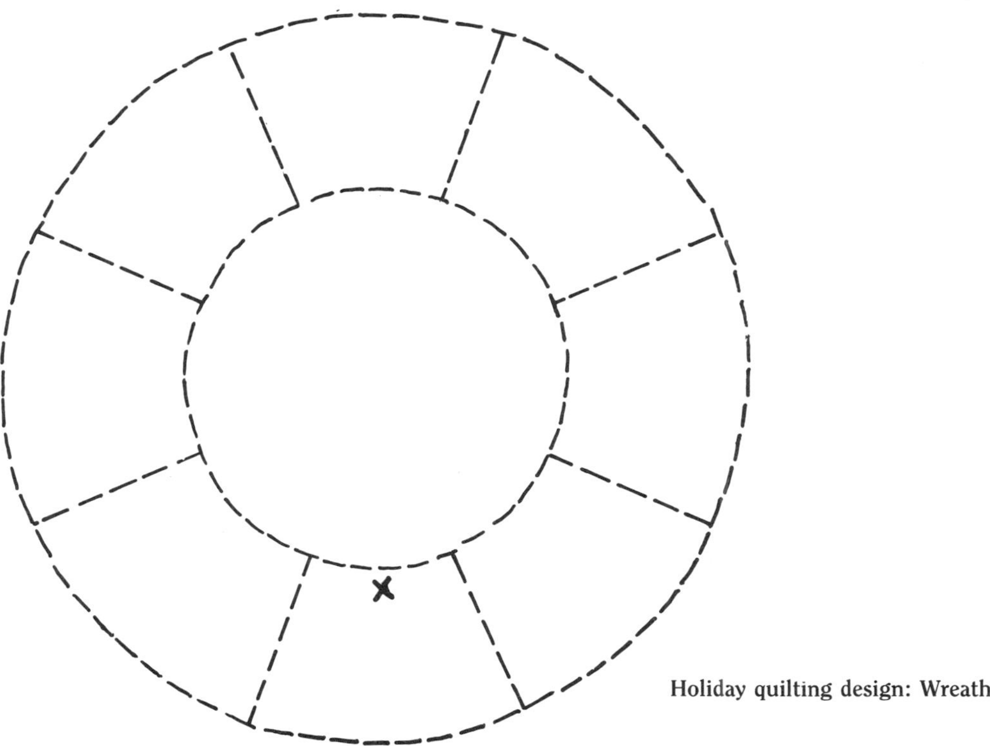

Holiday quilting design: Wreath

Holiday quilting design: Reindeer

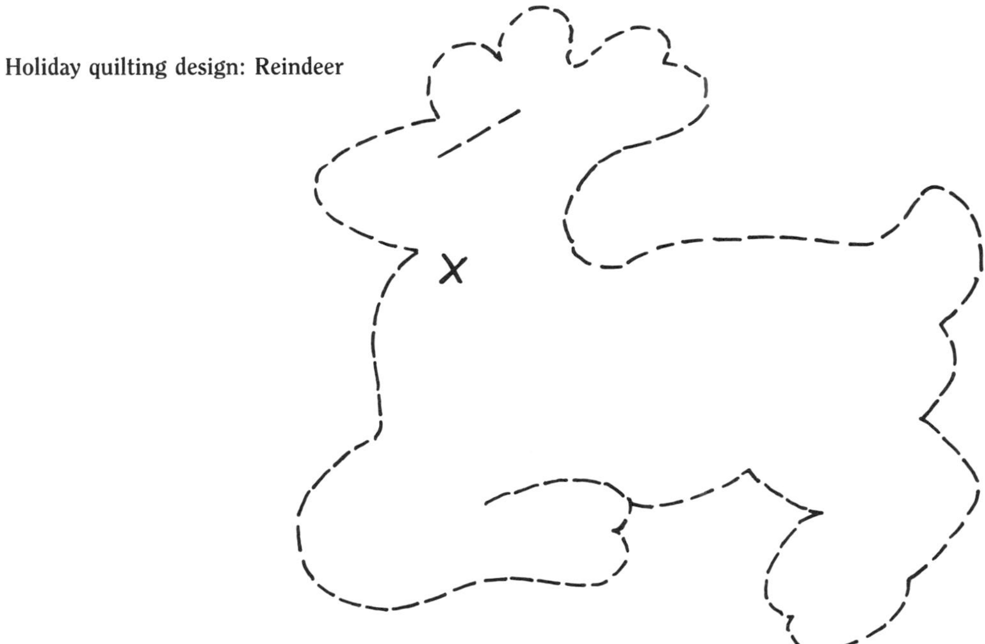

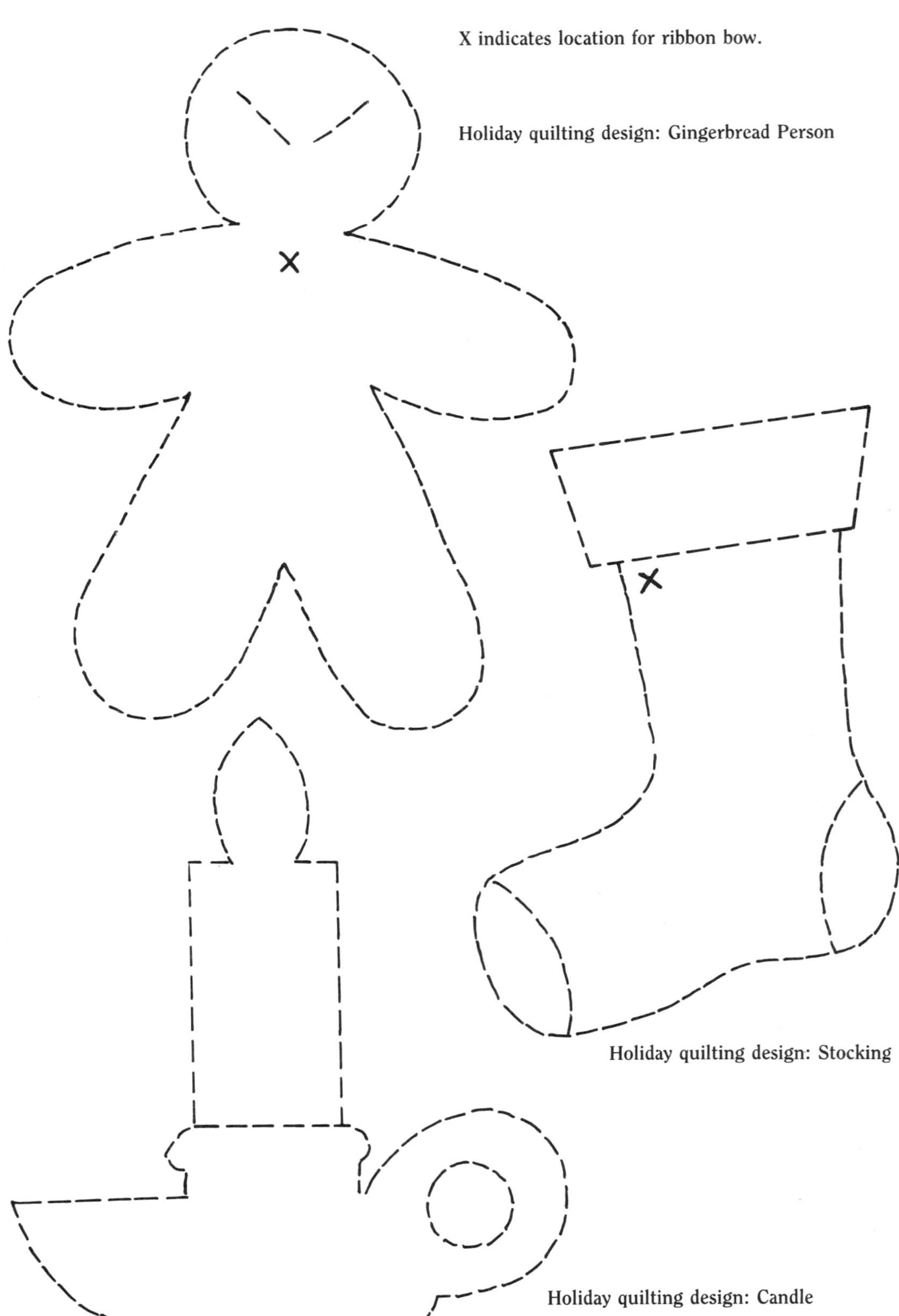

X indicates location for ribbon bow.

Holiday quilting design: Gingerbread Person

Holiday quilting design: Stocking

Holiday quilting design: Candle